D1267080

TREASURE!

Richard Knight's

TREASURE!

The True Story

of His Extraordinary

Quest

for Captain Kidd's Cache

by

Glenys Roberts

VIKING

VIKING

Penguin Books Ltd, Harmondsworth, Middlesex, England
Viking Penguin Inc., 40 West 23rd Street, New York, New York 10010, U.S.A.
Penguin Books Australia Ltd, Ringwood, Victoria, Australia
Penguin Books Canada Limited, 2801 John Street, Markham, Ontario,
Canada L3R 1B4
Penguin Books (N.Z.) Ltd, 182–190 Wairau Road, Auckland 10, New Zealand

First published 1986

Typeset in Linotron 202 Palatino

Typeset, printed and bound in Great Britain by
Hazell Watson and Viney Ltd
Member of the BPCC Group
Aylesbury, Bucks

British Library Cataloguing in Publication Data
Roberts, Glenys
Richard Knight's treasure!: the true story of his
extraordinary quest for Captain Kidd's cache
1. Kidd, William   2. Treasure-trove
I. Title   II. Roberts, Glenys
810.4'53   G525
ISBN 0-670-80761-3

Contents

Foreword

Richard Knight started to tell his extraordinary story in 1982. By then he had already been to Hon Tre Lon, the Grand Pirate Island of the South China Seas, on a mission which nobody thought possible, to find the lost pirate treasure of Captain Kidd. He told how he unearthed Kidd's secret cache after 300 years, what it was and what it looked like and why no one else had ever been able to decipher its location from Kidd's own map. He told too how he had discovered a second cache and that there was a third and fourth.

Even while he was telling it he was planning to return to the place on the remote island off Vietnam. He was arrested and his mission thoroughly investigated by the Vietnamese authorities. When he was released from a squalid jail sentence a year later he started to tell me the whole story in detail – in fits and starts, over the telephone, face to face in pubs and in the Penguin offices in the King's Road, and incredible as it is I have written it down with all the evidence exactly as he gave it to me.

Richard is the sort of man who has almost been extinguished in the late twentieth century, a free spirit whose existence seems improbable from within the confines of the office, the family or the bureaucratic procedures which discipline day-to-day life for the most part nowadays. It seems quite possible on meeting him that Captain Kidd himself has been reincarnated to tell his own story of where he buried his treasure and how it all came about. The story is so refreshing, Knight's approach so unorthodox, I was determined it should be told.

I want to acknowledge David Mitchell's book *Pirates*, in which Richard got his first taste of Captain Kidd, Rupert Furneaux's *The Money Pit Mystery*, which first put him on the scent of a solution, and *Pirates of the Eastern Seas* by Captain A. G. Course and *Victims of Piracy* by Evelyn Berckman, which both gave me the taste of the period in which Kidd was operating.

Glenys Roberts
1985

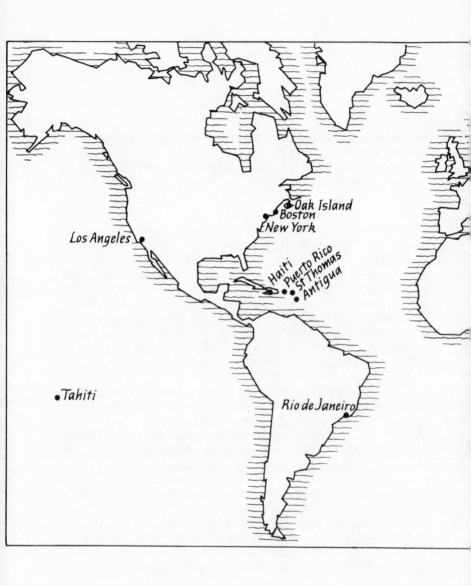

Oak Island
Boston
New York

Los Angeles

Haiti Puerto Rico
       St Thomas
       Antigua

Tahiti

Rio de Janeiro

Surat

Goa
Malabar
Coast

Bay
of
Bengal

Bangkok

Ho Chi Minh City (Saigon)

South China Sea

Hon Tre Ion

Straits of Malacca

Sumatra

Singapore

Madagascar

Sydney

Auckland

Dedicated by Richard Knight

to

Arthur Haynes

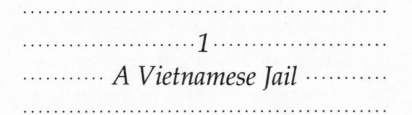

1

A Vietnamese Jail

'Tell me exactly what happened back there, Richard. Just how much do you know about treasure island?'

The speaker was Fred Graham. We were locked together in a darkened prison cell sixteen foot square in the middle of Vietnam. Every morning he asked me the same question, every evening, and several times in between. Fred was an insistent fellow agog with youthful curiosity. I suppose I couldn't blame him. He was only nineteen. He came from San Francisco. I came from Worthing in England. He knew practically nothing about me, yet he had been shut up for six months in Saigon for accompanying me on a hazardous expedition – the adventure of a lifetime. At this point in time I couldn't tell him any more than I had told the Vietnamese security officials at their repeated interrogations. It was reasonable to suppose those interrogations were not over. I didn't want him to betray anything involuntarily and get us both into worse trouble than we were already. So I said nothing. The silence hung between us like an impenetrable curtain. We had both spent our time in solitary confinement before being put together a few weeks previously. Then I had longed for a companion and the sound of another English-speaking voice, but now I grew desperate for my solitude again. I am sure Fred did too.

When they first turned the key on me in Rach Gia prison, all those months before, I had been locked in a cell about six by eight with no one but rats and cockroaches for company. We had been arrested, then hustled and prodded by the Red Guards all the way from Hon Tre Lon, an island in the middle of the South China Seas off the Vietnamese coast. We were terrific objects of curiosity, for they had not seen a westerner in these remote parts since the Americans left after the Vietnam war. When they took us to the local guardhouse in the tiny island hamlet, children and villagers crowded round to have a look. One of the village elders could remember a bit of French. 'Pourquoi vous êtes ici?' he kept demanding in an unfamiliar accent. I could just about understand him, for at one time I had lived in Paris with my French wife. The guards too were beside themselves with curiosity. What were we doing now in their part of the world? There had been no English, no Americans, few French, only Russians and Eastern Europeans anywhere in Vietnam for about eight years.

It was soon obvious that whatever answer I gave in this island outpost of the Socialist Republic of Vietnam it would not satisfy them. Our presence needed explaining to higher authority. At dead of night they bundled me into a small boat along with Fred and took us twelve miles through the darkness to the mainland port of Hatien. From there the boat proceeded up an inland canal between darkened fields.

It was a slow, anxious trip broken only by inexplicable and interminable delays which sapped our nerves, and from time to time by the menacing laughter of the guards. I am an actor by profession, with a lot of experience in comedy, and my natural instinct right from the beginning had been to try and make them laugh. When they offered me a glass of water in the guardhouse I gargled with it, and the barefoot ragged children of the village had responded like children the world over. But now, well within their territory and surrounded by armed soldiers, I wasn't feeling quite as confident. I was hungry and thirsty and they had confiscated all our possessions. We half lay, half sat on the bottom of the old boat, often with hands tied behind our backs, while the cockroaches crawled out of the timbers in the dark and walked all over us. With my hands out of action there was nothing I could do to keep them off. When I tried to speak a little French to my captors I discovered they spoke none at all, unlike the fellow in the village, and though I had once tried to learn a little Vietnamese, under these circumstances it disappeared completely. I decided

2

not to try and summon it up for fear they might think I knew more than I was saying.

For most of the trip we were bound at the wrists, and made to respond to their orders at gun-point. Even when they untied us and offered cigarettes I was overcome by the feeling they might be granting a final request. As it got light I peered over the gunwales and tried to make out where I was. I had studied the map of Vietnam for about four years now, and I had a good idea that they would take us to the provincial capital of Rach Gia. For the most part we were in open agricultural country where rice was the main crop. Every time we passed a village the inhabitants lined up on the banks of the waterway to stare at our progression, and the canal was narrow enough for me to gaze right into their blank inscrutable faces. The Vietnamese can be a beautiful people, but their menfolk can have some of the cruellest features in the world, especially if they come from the North. When we finally got to Rach Gia and stopped at a police station the officers came and went and stared again. It was a relief whenever we started moving.

This time a car came to take us to our final destination for the time being, a Vietnamese prison which, judging from the cultured nature of the other inmates, was for political prisoners. The metal doors of the main gate swung open and we entered a small courtyard about twenty foot square. Fred and I were each given a stool and made to sit in separate corners as if we were schoolboys, but we feared much more than a beating as we waited in silence for about an hour before being led into another courtyard off the smaller one. This, the main exercise yard of the prison, was the size of a tennis court, with small bare concrete cells leading off it. One of them was to be mine.

In those first days of solitary confinement I had plenty of time to wonder what would be my fate and what crime, if any, we had committed. In western terms we had illegally entered a country's territory with the intention of stealing property belonging to that country. But in Communist eyes – who knew what their interpretation might be? The atmosphere in the courtyard, which I could see through a small grille cut in my door, was shambolic and difficult to interpret. Everywhere there seemed to be young children. They slept and played in a huge dormitory cell block with the women and spilled out into the courtyard during the day to wash clothes at a little well or to exercise. The scene was watched constantly by guards leaning against the opposite walls who had the menacing habit of picking up sticks and swishing them in the dust at their feet. Often a guard's face would appear at the grilled window of my cell. Most of them were leering, hard and even insulting, but one spoke a little French, put on a kind face and seemed to wish me well.

In another dormitory cell block boys over the age of twelve shared with the men. I was certain from their manner and their bearing that these male prisoners were educated people, doctors perhaps who had not wanted to help the régime. The idea that such people could be behind bars was not a reassuring one and I was not allowed to contemplate it for long without my fears being aroused even further.

Three hours after I arrived an offering of a grizzled sandwich filled with stringy meat was followed by the arrival of uniformed and armed guards who pushed open the door of my cell and marched me down a long alleyway. I was sure the sandwich had been my last meal and that I would be shot like a dog in the lane, but the ordeal was by no means over yet. I was being taken to the interview block, where, in a bare interrogation room, furnished only with a desk and chair, some plain-clothes officers were waiting to receive me, including an interpreter who spoke English. At first the questions they asked appeared fairly straightforward: name, age, country of origin, profession, where we set out from, what equipment we had brought with us; but they never seemed satisfied with the answers at their 'investigative interviews', as they called them later on.

If I had ever thought otherwise it became obvious soon enough that the language barrier was the least of my troubles. There was no explaining myself to them, whatever language we used.

'Where have you come from?'

'What are you doing here?'

4

'How long had you been there?'

'What time did you arrive on the island?'

'Which political party do you belong to?'

These and many other questions were repeated again and again for two hours on end at least every two days, though the authorities never established a pattern that I could rely upon. Sometimes they offered me tea in oriental fashion, in a little cup without a saucer, sometimes even a cigarette, but always they wanted to know why had I come and who had sent me. Once they photographed me and took fingerprints, and often they asked me questions about my life, warning me beforehand that any discrepancies in my answers from day to day would be viewed most gravely and would be punished. I took them seriously and feared for my life. What a ludicrous end it would have been to the career of an entertainer, not being able to remember whether I had skated in the Blackpool ice show of 1968 or 1970, but I was in no position to appreciate the irony of it.

I ate their thin soups and drank their boiled water; I lost two stone in weight over the next few weeks and tossed and turned all night on the board which served as a bed, listening to the scamperings and squeakings of the rats in the courtyard gutter and wrapping my mosquito net close round me, tucking the ends under the wooden board. The net was a blessing which I had not had at first. I hate mosquitoes even more than most people do, and they were one of the plagues I had to accept during my expedition to the Far East. But the net was proof against more than mosquitoes for there the large rats in the courtyard liked to get in under the door and bite my nose or any other part which happened to be exposed. This happened several times.

The depersonalization of prison life continued. They confiscated my clothes on the first day and substituted for them a regulation pyjama suit. Every day another prisoner came to slop out the plastic chamberpot in the corner of my cell and fill my plastic water-pot with boiled water. He would also douse me with a hose for five minutes; but there were no luxuries to prison life like razor blades. It was uncomfortably hot in my cell, with a bare electric light bulb burning day and night over the door. Soon I began to feel that any excuse to leave the cell was welcome, even the interrogations. My frank answers to their questions obviously bewildered them so much they called for new reinforcements from the Department of National Security in Saigon to delve more deeply into our circumstances. It was obvious to me that the country's whole security system was probing our case. In the first two weeks new faces were always appearing at the investigative interviews. These new people asked the same questions.

'What was your real reason for being on the island?'

'We do not believe you. You must tell the truth,' they thundered. On one fearful occasion they introduced a 'hard' man, a professional tough trained in the bullying technique. While most of the officials were small, thin and wiry, he was a big man. The face twisted into the hard cynical approach and he bawled at me in Vietnamese: 'We must have the truth from you.' The interpreter translated. He spat out his questions in the same aggressive manner and pointed accusations at me. 'Do you realize the political situation between our two countries?' 'Yes.' I was stammering by now but I managed to say that I had no political or military motive for being on the island. Fortunately that was the last time I met him. I did not sleep well that night.

They laid little traps for me, finding an amiable English-speaking prisoner to waylay me as I washed my clothes at the courtyard well. 'Are you really English?' he asked. It was becoming obvious that they thought I was American, or at least in the pay of the Americans, for I had told them I had spent time in California. 'I was told you worked with the British Embassy?' my new friend said conversationally. I always told them the same truth. I was an actor by profession. I had gone on to the stage straight from school at sixteen. I specialized in pantomime, summer theatre and comedy routines. On one occasion I mentioned working in a show in Edinburgh. 'Scotland – yes?' said the interpreter. 'That's an English colony, isn't it?' Whether they believed what I said or not, they asked me to make a voice recording of an elementary English book, ostensibly for use in their primary schools. It was called *Mr Smith Goes to Market*. They listened gravely as I did so and then said: 'Thank you very much, Mr Knight.' They also asked me to sing a song from my repertoire. In the circumstances I rejected the idea of *California Here I Come*, hesitated over *It's a Long Way to Tipperary* and decided on *Who Were You With Last Night?* There was no laughter and no applause when I got to the end of it.

In those first weeks in prison I was glad when I occasionally caught a glimpse of Fred, who was separated from me by two cells. I nodded and winked discreetly to him on the way to and from our separate interrogations. He seemed to be bearing up well, but I knew it must have been a terrifying end to an adventure he had been apprehensive about right from the start. Fred was a photo-journalist. He wanted to write about a good story. He didn't necessarily want to live it in the way this one was turning out. He hadn't anticipated it ending in this way, any more than I had.

One day Fred and I found ourselves together in the prison offices. The authorities gave us our own clothes back and said we were leaving the prison. For a minute my hopes rose irrationally and I thought we were being released. The truth was much less encouraging. They promised us better conditions and they asked us to put in our own requests for food and drink and to communicate any problems about the conditions of our detention. They even promised that we would be released eventually when their inquiries were complete. But the fact of the matter for the time being was that we were simply being transferred to another place of detention, and that place was in the capital, Ho Chi Minh City – formerly Saigon. There were two cars waiting in the courtyard to take us separately to Saigon, each under the guard of three plain-clothes security men.

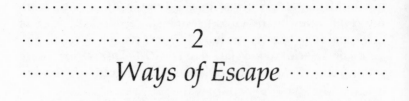

2
Ways of Escape

It was a day's journey to the capital, and I was to get to know the road well over the months that followed. Now for the first time I had a chance to have a good look at the Vietnamese countryside, which I had studied not only on maps but on satellite photographs for the last two years. We had been far too busy before they arrested us on the island to enjoy the surroundings. We were still in flat farming country, populated by poor people, lined with paddyfields and broken by the occasional village. Peasants were working the fields in conical hats and pyjama suits, and flocks of ducks waddled down the centre of the roads. The graves and tombs seemed to be dotted around in the open fields, not enclosed in cemeteries.

Twice during the long journey I contemplated escaping, for after a three-hour drive we came to the Mekong River at about six in the evening when dusk was falling. We had to cross the delta twice at Can Toi and My Toi, and once the car was on the ferry the guards left me alone in it and wandered off for a smoke and a walk. The local Vietnamese peered through the windows of the car, thinking perhaps that I was Russian or French, and it occurred to me for the first time then that though I was one of the few foreigners who had visited this part of the country I was not the only foreigner in Vietnam and that I might go undetected long enough to find an escape route back to the West. On the outskirts of Con Toi the two cars pulled up and our guards let us get out to stretch our legs. Then they produced some bread, Vietnamese sausage and coconuts. They seemed to be waiting for something, but I could not tell what. I gazed across the open countryside and the ricefields and wondered if despite all our cultural differences there was a common streak of humanity. Did they know this was going to be our last night in the open for a very long time? Whether they did or not, that is what proved to be the case.

In the end I gave up my notions of escape and pinned my hopes on being released as the authorities had promised. Though the detention was to be long and tedious I had not exactly landed in their country unprepared for the event of imprisonment if disaster struck. Sooner or later I believed the letter I had written in Bangkok before setting out on my adventure would fall on friendly ears. In fact it was to be a long time before anyone did anything at all.

Back home the *Daily Mail* first carried the story of my arrest six weeks after it happened on 16 June 1983. My mother was not informed by the Foreign Office that I had indeed been captured until a couple of weeks after that, and though she kept in touch with their Mrs Clay through all the months I was in jail, the wheels of bureaucracy in both countries ground slowly. On the very first day of arrest I had asked to contact the British Embassy. I did so again about a month later, but so far no permission had been given and nothing had happened. Two months after I had been captured, the authorities in England were still trying to find out where I was being held, what were the details of my charge, and whether there would be a trial. As far as they were concerned I was lost in Vietnam, and if I had known this at the time it would certainly have added to my depression. As it was, I was apprehensive but hopeful on the road to Saigon.

I sat back and studied the country once more. It was no longer possible to distinguish the ravages of time from those of war, but it was obvious that Vietnam had not been able to make much of an economic recovery. The buildings, once beautiful examples of French colonial architecture, were longing for a coat of paint and clearly none had been applied since the Americans left. Throughout my stay in Saigon the authorities were careful that I should not have any opportunity to study the city by daylight.

This time we arrived in the outskirts at about ten p.m. and drew up a little later in the courtyard of a French-style three-storey building with shutters at the windows. My guards disappeared and returned with a man in a long

white coat who had a most hideous appearance, the cruel
face, high cheek-bones and drawn-in cheeks of the typical
Northern Vietnamese. Whoever the man was, I was not in
a hospital but in another prison. The building was about
fifty years old and had obviously had certain amenities
when it was first built, which led me to conclude it was a
prison for French officers. My third-floor cell was about
twelve foot square, this time furnished with a bureau and
chair of cheap but solid wood and a bed of wooden planks
standing about eighteen inches from the ground. It had a
straw mattress and a mosquito net already suspended from
wooden poles like a primitive four-poster. The paint was
peeling from the walls, but it had started off life a pleasant
pale blue and the floor was made of coloured tiles. I even
had a private bathroom, about twelve foot long, with western facilities, including a square footbath.

That is the good news; the bad is that the bath was permanently blocked up, and the circular bathroom window
which had once let in a good deal of light was covered with
a thick coat of yellow paint on the outside. I was never
given any work in the cell and became so lethargic I
couldn't even bother to lift the mop which was kept under
the bed. A fine layer of dust began to cover everything. A
25-watt bulb glowed intermittently a yard to the right of
the door. It was high up on the wall and there was nothing
to be done but wait for the authorities to switch it on and
off.

The bulb was very important to me because the window
was grilled over with fixed slats which left my cell in permanent gloom. I could just about peer down through the bottom slats into the exercise yard beneath and see the young
Viet Cong guards and sometimes even their wives, who
were free to come and go. I could make out a few vehicles
parked to the right of my cell, and the personnel kitchen
and restaurant by the main gate on my left.

The gate set me thinking about ways of escape again. I
calculated that if I hid in the bathroom when the guards
entered my cell, I could nip out behind them, through the
open door and lie low in the corridors on the ground floor
until the gate was opened for one of the cars. I would follow

10

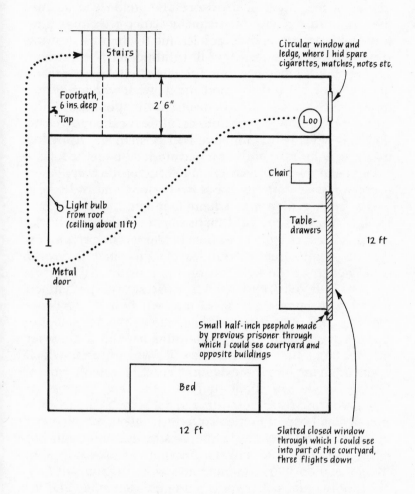

*Richard Knight's plan of his cell in his first prison
in Ho Chi Minh City (Saigon)*

it and then I would have to hide out in the streets of Saigon. This would be tricky but I thought that if I knocked at someone's door there was a good chance they would agree to shelter me. Most of the Saigonese were dead against the Communist régime, because they could remember how free and easy life had been in South Vietnam when the Americans were there. They all regretted the 'liberation' in 1974, as the Vietnamese now call it. But it was a big risk – not only for me but for them. Anyone found sheltering me would have certainly incurred the displeasure of the authorities, and two years' prison sentence themselves no doubt; besides which the gate was permanently guarded by a sentry in front of the restaurant. I gave up the idea.

Opposite me there was an office block which appeared to contain classrooms for the soldiers, and to the right there was a small garden area which soon had me longing for fresh air. In the courtyard there were little flocks of ducks and chickens, obviously destined for the cooking pot, but they all seemed freer than I was. For the worst of it was I could never see the sky.

It was 1 July 1983, and when the solid steel door slammed shut I was imprisoned in permanent twilight for nine months, the only variety provided by the trips to the interrogation room. Fred had a similar but rather better cell, for some unaccountable reason, with shutters which opened, giving him some daylight and a view of the street. Otherwise we were both subject to the same régime. At 7.30 a young Vietnamese girl arrived with breakfast on a tray, a small cup of French coffee and sugar, a boiled egg or brioche and a banana. She was pleasant enough but entirely businesslike, always greeting me the same way: 'Bonjour, monsieur, comment allez-vous aujourd'hui?'

Every two days she would bring me cigarettes, and if I ran out she sometimes supplemented my rations. She also brought me sleeping pills at my request, two at a time, but they were horribly weak and next to useless in curing my restless nights. They started at 8.30 after dinner. At 11.30 in the morning she would bring me lunch. And then the interrogations would start, sometimes in a similar cell a couple of doors along, sometimes in the interrogation

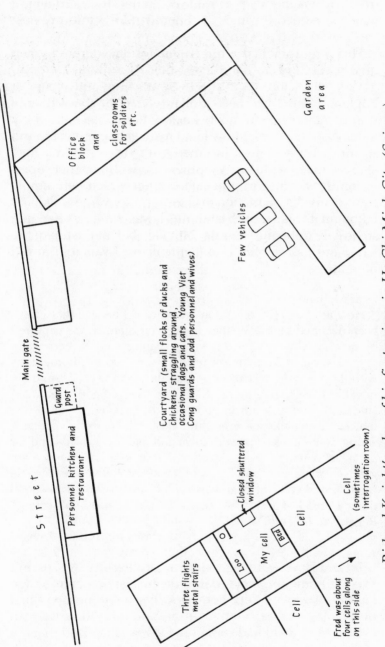

Richard Knight's plan of his first prison in Ho Chi Minh City (Saigon)

room, where my eyes would be blinded by the daylight which streamed through the open windows and my nostrils teased by the fresh air.

This time they had a bizarre line of questioning; when did I last see my mother, they wanted to know. They found it very suspicious that she lived on the south coast of England while I had been globe-trotting for about twenty years. They were curious to know where I had earned my money and especially how I had managed to travel around so much on a limited income. After three months they allowed me to write to my mother – under their strict supervision. It was a scruffy pencilled letter which held ample signs of my disorientation to those who knew me well. First I thought it was a month later than it was, time was hanging so heavily upon me. I wrote '24th October' at the top of the letter and had to alter it to 'September'. I was told to put no address.

Dear Mother

How are you? [I wrote] You have heard I believe that I have been detained by the Vietnamese Government. I was captured by them on the 16th June at Kiang Giang province, because of my violation of Vietnamese territory and taking photographs without permission. [The authorities dictated the charge and the next bits of encouraging news.] I have received good treatment since I arrived and am in good health. I receive good meals, which are usually macaroni and meat slices, fresh vegetable soups, sometimes chips with meat and fish. I get salads and for breakfast usually a glass of coffee and an egg and bread. I am given cigarettes and smoke about ten a day. I have a reasonable room and am alright healthwise. I have just been given something to read at last. The Vietnam Courier and another one. Regards to Jill and Dave,

With much love, Richard

Jill and Dave were my sister and brother-in-law. I hadn't lived at home for years, but to be imprisoned in a foreign jail can make you very homesick. For three months I had no reading matter of any sort and nothing to write with either. Now that I had something to read I realized that my eyesight had been deteriorating during the months in jail, and it was a strain to concentrate for more than short periods at a time. The *Vietnam Courier* was a politically orientated news bulletin about Vietnam published monthly in English. It was a thin read, with no news of England, and I half-heartedly wended my way through it. A couple of days later I was given two books on Russian fairy tales which were hardly more appropriate. It was to be some time before my own copy of *Three Men in a Boat* was returned to me together with Lauren Bacall's autobiography *By Myself*, the two books I had taken along on my trip. Meanwhile I eked out the cigarettes. I would light the same one maybe three or four times a day, realizing that I depended as much on the ritual for something to do as the smoke itself.

The letter in which I gave my mother this sparse picture of my imprisonment was sent by the prison authorities to the British Embassy in Hanoi, who sent it on to the Foreign Office in October 1983; my mother received it two weeks later, when I had already been held for four months. She told me later that she wrote back as soon as she heard the letter had been received in London, without waiting to see its content, but that letter, like so many others sent by friends in England, failed to reach me. She wrote again less than three weeks later, and sent a Christmas card which was given to me several weeks after. The illusion of communication helped to keep up my mother's spirits.

By now Richard Luce had been in touch with her. He was then Minister of State at the Foreign Office whose special area of responsibility included South East Asia. By chance he was also the Member of Parliament for our own home constituency. One assurance in his letter of 21 October gave her particular encouragement. 'You can rest assured', he wrote, 'that the Embassy will continue to press the Vietnamese to let them know where your son is being held. As soon as this is established, they will arrange Consular access so that they can ensure for themselves that he is being treated in accordance with normal Consular practice.' She was very encouraged at the time and wanted to share the good news with me that Le Van Bang, the Third Secretary at the Vietnamese Embassy in London, had

assured her on the telephone that I would be released without a trial before Christmas.

Van Bang's correspondence with my mother suggested
that I was not even in prison. He repeated the accusation,
which was true up to a point, that 'Mr R. Knight had
entered Vietnamese territory illegally. He had violated
Vietnamese sovereignty and security. He was caught while
carrying fire-arms, munition, cameras, walkie-talkie. Mr
Knight, however, once detained, has received well-treat-
ment . . . Although Mr Knight showed disregard for Vietnamese Law and Order, he had not been brought to Court.
His case was settled at an administrative level without
imprisonment.' Van Bang included with his letter a transcript of an announcement on Radio Vietnam on 23
November. When my mother saw me on television on New
Year's Day playing a drunk in evening dress in the Jacques
Tati film *Playtime* she was sure she would see me shortly in
real life, for the transcript read:

Richard Knight, British citizen and Frederich [*sic*] Graham,
American citizen, who have been found illegally infiltrating into
Vietnam's territorial waters have been ordered to leave Vietnam
as soon as possible according to a decision on November 23rd
1983 by the People's Committee of the Kian Giang Province at
the Southernmost part of Vietnam.

In fact the frontier guards and people of Kian Giang on 10th
and 18th June 1983 have discovered two motor-boats infiltrating
illegally into the territorial waters offshore near the province
coast. The occupants of these boats were precisely Richard
Knight, 47 and Frederich Graham, 19, British and American
citizens respectively. They were equipped with arms,
munitions, cameras, photo machines, walkie-talkies and other
equipments.

Before irrefutable proofs Richard Knight and Frederich Graham admitted before the Vietnamese authorities that they had
committed acts at the expense of the national security of Vietnam.

On 23rd of November the People's Committee of Kian Giang
decided to fine these two offenders a sum of money and
obliged them to leave Vietnam's territory as soon as possible.

The boat and technical materials used by the two foreigners were confiscated.

Richard Knight and Frederich Graham received humanitarian treatment during their detention.

In the interests of accuracy, Van Bang and the Vietnamese authorities in the country itself were wrong about two things. Firstly I was not carrying arms, and neither was I endangering their security. In fact the two Thais had foolishly brought along handguns with them which the Vietnamese picked up on the mother ship. All I had was a toy plastic pistol which was later to amuse Vietnamese security.

Secondly my arrival in their country had no political significance whatsoever. Over the weeks I became adept at answering their political questions.

'What do you think of our government?'

'It is your country and your government.'

'What do you think of us?'

'Everyone is an individual.'

'What are your politics?'

'I have no interest in politics.'

'What do you think of Mrs Thatcher?'

'I think she is probably doing her job to the best of her ability.'

There was much talk about imperial aggression, for they were reluctant to believe that I had no interest in politics since I had landed uninvited on their island on a mission which was only known to me. I was kept going throughout by the idea that I would soon be released and that I had a lot to look forward to when I was.

For the first month I did nothing in the cell. I rested and spent most of the time worrying about these interrogations and trying to prepare myself for the difficult or sensitive questions they still might ask. Then it obviously became necessary to work on methods of keeping going during the long boring hours of solitary confinement.

Sometimes I imagined I was in a little Belgian hotel in Bruges which I had once visited. The hotel was overbooked but the manager was full of continental bonhomie and had given me a top attic room while waiting for a vacancy. There were inconveniences. The window was jammed, for instance, but it was better than being on the streets. Sometimes I imagined I was convalescing. The hotel waitress brought up my meals three times a day because I insisted on privacy. I called it the Hôtel de Liège.

Sometimes I imagined I was on a cruise. I had worked on boats as an entertainer and I knew you could feel imprisoned on the high seas. I imagined I was eating luxurious five-course meals in the ship's restaurant. I learned to perform contortions so I could partly submerge myself in the blocked two-foot-square footbath and pretend I was taking a dip in the ship's pool.

I played imaginary rounds of golf at Finchley Golf Club in North London. I had played there from time to time but had no handicap. In my cell I became an expert. I could have taken on Ballesteros.

In my mind I kept going on a recurring visit to Blackpool, scene of many a happy summer season in my life. I started doing exercises twice a day and walking and running set distances, five hundred yards, a thousand, one mile. The most I covered in one day was three and a half miles. I measured the floor exactly by lying full length on it. Then I jogged round and round my cell or across it diagonally until I had completed the distance I set myself.

I thought about the parts I would play when I got out and the films I would make. Sometimes I worked on sketches. I was given matches for my cigarettes and I would line up the burnt ones out of sight on the window ledge to keep track of the date. If I lost track I was always reminded by the documents I had to sign confessing what I had been doing on the island.

Always the interrogations continued.

'Who is your contact in the British government?'

'I haven't got a contact.'

'Who do you know in Thailand?' They knew I had come from there.

'I have no special friends.'

Then for one terrible month the interrogations ceased. Now I had nothing to look forward to. I practised comic walks round the perimeter of my cell and continued with my exercises, but it seemed pointless doing them for more than twenty minutes twice a day. I designated the four corners of my cell as quite different areas as if I was living in a large mansion and invented rules about what must be done in each one of them. One was a comic corner where I had to do something funny. One was a religious corner where I prayed. One was to consider the future, another the past. And though the authorities refused me reading matter and writing materials when I asked, I had managed to save one piece of badly milled brown paper from those interrogation sessions where I had been asked to answer written questions in a separate room. I had even managed to hide a ballpoint pen.

I used the paper and the pen to work out a winning roulette system and a blackjack system. I made myself a deck of cards too and played patience, crib and poker in the bathroom out of sight of the grille in the door, for I was terrified they would punish me for having these unofficial divertissements. I kept my cards in an empty cigarette packet.

These were terrible times, with my solitude only punctuated by the screamings of other inmates. Of course I imagined they were being tortured, but on reflection I think they were only bored to distraction like myself. In these circumstances my thoughts occasionally turned to suicide, and I passed the time perfecting four different methods. I could drown myself in the footbath, hang myself with the mosquito net, stab or cut myself with the knife which was left at mealtimes to cut my food; or I could take an overdose of the sleeping pills which I had collected over the months. The lack of exercise had made it difficult to sleep but they were reluctant to hand out sleeping pills very often. So I asked for them about once a week and experimented with their strength. In fact they weren't very strong at all, but I had collected thirty-seven and I figured this would be enough. At one point I even went on hunger strike for a couple of days.

19

I gave it up for the simple reason that I was hungry, but I tried it twice more before my eventual release. At least it brought the officials running immediately and prompted them to show some concern. So life barely went on, and it took five months for the Vietnamese authorities to get round to any positive mention of what would become of me.

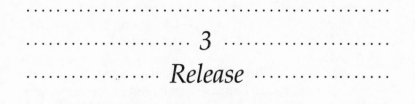

One day about four months into my sentence I was handed a letter which had been sent from the British Embassy in Hanoi two weeks previously. It stated that the British Consul had heard of my disappearance in the Gulf of Thailand in local Thai press reports. The Embassy was trying to arrange to see me. It was the first conclusive evidence that in fact the outside world did know of our situation. Prior to that letter I had no idea if anybody knew we were being held in Vietnam, hence my concern that even after four months we could still simply 'disappear'.

Then one day I was taken into the interview room and told I was about to be thrown out of Vietnam. Before I could express my delight the interpreter told me there would be a trial first, after which a fine would have to be paid. A little one-sided haggling went on to determine the amount. 'Can you afford 500 dollars?' he asked. I knew these oriental bargains, so I said no. 'Oh, well, it may be 1,000 dollars,' he countered. 'It could even be as much as 5,000 – or even 10,000.' Two days later they said: 'Yes it has been decided you must pay 20,000 dollars – for two men.' Paper was then provided for me to write to my mother and friends back home to ask for this amount. I decided to put all in one letter to the British Consul in Hanoi, who informed England. The news that the fine was so large was a terrible blow. I didn't know anyone who had that sort of money to spare except the man who had funded my trip to Vietnam in the first place, and he was staying strangely silent. My mother, my father, who was divorced from her when I was a child, their friends were powerless to help. My mother spent her whole time tuned to the radio in England where there were conflicting reports of my fate. One day they announced on Radio Sussex in the morning I had been deported to Bangkok for medical reasons, only to change their story in the afternoon. News of the fine remained unhappily constant and the Foreign Office tried in vain to get it reduced.

Bad news always brings sympathizers, and mine was no exception. Mrs Laura Lancaster from Rye, whose son was imprisoned in Thailand for a year, confirmed Van Bang's explanation for the fine. In her son's case his fine was to pay for all expenses arising from his unwilling detention in their country. The Lancasters even had to pay for his keep throughout, though the whole fine amounted to about a quarter of mine. The longer the Lancaster family were unable to raise the money the more the fine grew. Our fine was a flat fee. It amounted not to a fine but to a ransom. Mrs Lancaster suggested that my mother contact Amnesty International in London, which had arranged the release of her son, to see if it might advance the money for the fine. This gave my mother hope, but it was not a solution: Amnesty is only able to help political prisoners and this of course was not at all my situation. Other people did their little bit. My mother even contacted Equity, the actors' union, and its president of that year, Peter Finch, started to look into my case. When my plight was told on coast-to-coast American television a cheque arrived for £5 towards the fine from Mr and Mrs Stanley Watson and their daughter Diane. Stanley Watson was a magician with whom I had done a summer show in Minehead twenty years previously. My aunty Betty sent £10. Before my release they gave me a letter from her in which she mentioned several relatives. I was thoroughly interrogated as to who these people might be, their ages, professions, political parties. At the end of the letter she had written 'Puss is now 16 and will probably outlive me.' Naturally they wanted to know all about Puss and his political leanings, but I must say they did see the humour in it when I explained he was a cat.

The fund was increasing bit by bit. Later the Shoreham Rotary Club sent a donation. But there were cranks too. Someone in Brighton telephoned Radio Sussex to say he had been left some money and would send a cheque for

£6,000 immediately. It was a hoax. Someone else kept putting notes through my mother's letterbox asking to meet
her privately. When she refused to keep the appointment
without my brother-in-law the letters ceased. And there
were disappointments. An anonymous would-be donor
from Singapore wanted to be assured that the money
would be secure in the fund. He was assured but nothing
materialized.

Back in the prison they measured me for a striped blue
and white pyjama suit and seemed desperate that Fred and
I should think kindly of them and testify that we had been
well treated. They allowed us to celebrate New Year, which
was their special annual holiday instead of Christmas.
They even served us festive food. Towards the end of my
sentence they had even allowed me into the garden, for I
told them constantly I longed for fresh air and for daylight.
The 'garden' was a small, overgrown courtyard with a
banana tree and a table where I was allowed to sit and
smoke while the guard sat nearby. On subsequent outings
he brought a Vietnamese book which he shared with me,
although I could scarcely focus on the pictures because my
eyes had spent so long unaccustomed to bright light.

These outings took place twice a week for about three
weeks. The weather was hot and my guard even brought
out to me tumblers of natural orange juice with ice. He tried
to teach me Vietnamese by pointing at the birds, the table,
the chair, but I was purposely slow to learn. I didn't want to
encourage any misunderstandings, so I taught him English
words instead. On my third outing he brought a chess set.
I play the game reasonably well for a layman but he was
hot stuff and always beat me – till the last time, when I
turned the tables on him. I was never asked out into the
garden again. I often wondered whether my victory had
anything to do with it. Losing at chess seems to bring out
the worst in people, judging by the last Grand Tournament
in Russia. I took the renewed incarceration very badly but
there was something even better to look forward to than
the garden. Towards the very end of my imprisonment I
had a couple of proper sorties into the town to meet with

the British Consul or members of his staff. By now questions had begun to be answered back home.

One morning they came to get me before dawn. It was four a.m. and I remember it plainly. It was Saturday, 2 December 1983. Before it was light they had whisked me off to a hotel in Saigon to meet Philip Roberts, who was the British Consul in Hanoi. He had come down the night before, and was brought over from his hotel just after breakfast. For me it was a red letter day. I had had bacon and eggs served in my room at 7.30. I felt as if I was going home. A small interview room had been set up in the hotel and Roberts was shown into it with my interpreter Mr Lee and a photographer. I had already been told I was not allowed to reveal where I was being held prisoner, so our conversation was inevitably a bit stilted. I said: 'It is very nice to see an Englishman after all this time.' It was an understatement.

Roberts asked all the obvious questions about my health and frame of mind, formulating certain key queries in such a way that Lee for all his good English would find them too colloquial to understand properly. 'Have you been having hallucinations?' he asked me. I had to confess I had. 'Do you have a feeling your mind is wandering?' Again yes. At times it seemed possible that my food had been drugged to facilitate their questioning and increase my alienation. 'Are you allowed a doctor?' Indeed I was. 'Do you hear any unusual noises in jail?' he asked. This time I lied. 'No,' I said. I didn't want to tell him about the regular cries I heard from the Vietnamese prisoners. I imagined their ears were being boxed or that they were being tortured when they were interrogated. I was not ill-treated myself. We started to relax and even had some beer and cigarettes brought to us.

But Roberts had bad news. He had tried to contact the people back home in England whom I had mentioned in my letter and had had no success. He had also heard that the British Consul in Singapore was in contact with my backer, to whom I had posted a letter on the day of our departure, the letter I had intended as a fail-safe device if we did not return within two weeks. I had been so sure this man would help me in an emergency. He was the man under whose auspices I had made the journey to Vietnam in the first place, he was the man who stood to gain as much as I did by my efforts, the man whose backing had in a roundabout way actually put me into prison. Yet I learned he had refused to stand by me. He was contacted three or four times and he still refused to help. This preyed on me constantly over the next few weeks when I got back to my cell. Later he denied that he had ever received the letter, but I knew better.

I was allowed about one hour with Roberts at the time. He was a quiet man but likable and capable of thoughtful touches. As he was about to leave, he said 'You have taken photographs of Mr Knight for yourselves. Please may I have some photographs for myself?' They agreed, and later I learned he sent one to my mother, with the request by the Foreign Office for it not to be published. For me he had brought a carton of 555 cigarettes and four paperbacks in a plastic bag. The guards flipped through them to make sure nothing was concealed but I was allowed to keep them. I must have read each one of them a dozen times over the next few months. At the bottom of the small plastic bag was another larger one folded up. I had no idea why it was placed there, but to me it represented another way out, a fifth means of suicide if necessary. As we left I had one final question for Mr Roberts. 'How are Brighton doing in the League?' He regretted that he did not follow football – not as much as I regretted it. Then he left saying that now the Embassy had access to me he hoped that he or another official would be able to visit me every two weeks or so on their regular trips from Hanoi to Ho Chi Minh City.

It was an encouraging note on which to part and I was in a good frame of mind as I was abandoned to my own devices in my room till after dark. Even my guards seemed determined to turn a blind eye to discipline. When the waiter brought a mid-day meal to my room I asked him to bring several beers. He did and I spent a very pleasant time in a proper hotel room till eight o'clock at night, when I was driven back through the dark streets to my lonely cell.

In fact Roberts's hope of regular meetings was not to be

fulfilled and it turned into a bitter disappointment as weeks
went by without a further visit. That was the last time I saw
the Consul himself and it was nearly four months later that
I was able to see his Vice-Consul, Bob Webb, for lunch in
the same hotel. He was a more expansive man than
Roberts, but he did not know as much about Vietnam. He
had only been posted from Africa about a month before. In
a way that made us immediate allies in a strange land.
Webb had some good news and some bad. They still had
not gathered enough money for my release, but Buster
Gray, whom I vaguely remembered from my schooldays
in Shoreham, had started a fund on my behalf.

It had been a brainwave of my mother's to get in contact
with the old school enclosing newspaper cuttings about
my imprisonment. There was a new generation of teachers
there now, of course, but Mr Bruder, the ex-headmaster,
remembered me and although he was already eighty years
old he took an interest in the case. Buster was President
of the Old Boys Association and he had contacted him. It
started to come back to me. Buster, whose real name was
Edward, was the son of 'Monsewer' Eddie Gray of the
Crazy Gang. He lived in London, had become rather well
connected and still had the marvellous enthusiasm for life
he had had as a boy when he remembered we had had
many pranks together. His ebullience cheered my mother
up no end. He was constantly telephoning her and turning
up with the reassurance 'We will get Richard out by hook
or by crook.'

Every week he reported the state of the fund – now £300,
now it was 1000 dollars, now it was £1000. The school
arranged an auction in the college on behalf of my appeal
fund and Luke, a Chinese old boy, sent £50 from Hong
Kong. I was and still am deeply grateful to everyone who
contributed but it was a big blow when Webb told me he
was not exactly sure how much had been collected to date.
I sensed it was still very short of the sum required to get
me out of there.

All the same, lunch with Webb turned out to be a very
pleasant interlude. This time our conversation was moni-
tored by a female interpreter, and after the meal all the

security guards joined up with us to watch a one-and-a-half-hour Kung Fu video. At one point the interpreter asked me a loaded question: 'Mr Knight, would you say your stay in prison has been hell?' 'No,' I lied.

Like Roberts, Webb had brought some paperbacks for me to read in my cell. Things were indeed getting better. In fact the second time I met with Bob Webb he gave me the news that someone I had never known had offered to pay the balance of my fine. His name was Kenneth Crutchlow. He was an Englishman who was living in San Francisco and driving a taxi. I was too excited to wonder at the time what his interest was in me, especially as, once again, there was bad news to go with the good news. The Vietnamese government had now decided that they needed 300 dollars a month expenses on top of the fine. I had now been in the country so long that these expenses totalled 3,500 dollars, which Kenneth Crutchlow was not willing to pay.

Webb advised me to write to the Chairman of the Vietnamese Council of State asking for clemency; indeed he had brought along a typed letter to the gentleman for me to sign. In it was a plea to waive the additional fine just as Fred's had been waived two months previously. I would only find the outcome of this request six weeks later.

My guards asked often if my health was all right and when it wasn't they soon enough took me to hospital for an X-ray. Despite the inhospitable conditions in which I had lived for more than a year now I had been surprisingly well. I never had any reaction to the food, which was reasonable and just about sufficient, and the only testament to the airless conditions in which I lived was the constant presence of jungle foot, about which they were concerned enough to bring me cream. But at this time I had unaccountably developed a lump in my right chest which filled me with considerable concern. I was very anxious for proper X-rays and treatment in case it turned out to be malignant. My attitude proved conclusively that if ever I had entertained any notions to the contrary, I really did want to live. I had many things to do yet and the most important concerned their island. I had to get out of their clutches. The hospital doctor seemed unruffled by my symptoms but organized a succession of injections into my arm, administered back in my cell, promising me the growth would go away within three weeks.

It took considerably longer than that, by which time my mother had been informed and the British Consul tried to press for my release on compassionate grounds, but go away it did and my release took its normal course. Only the money counted in the end, for the trial had already been held and the outcome determined.

The 'trial' was fascinating. It was perhaps a formality to give the illusion of democracy, rather like Gaddafi's people's congresses in Libya. One fine day I was taken with Fred to Rach Gia, where we had first been held in Kiang Giang province, where Hon Tre Lon, the island where we had been found, was situated. The trial seemed the culmi-nation of their determination to wrench every conceivable benefit from our situation. It was certainly only a show trial in which my role was rehearsed ahead of time in the prison in Saigon.

I knew by now that the authorities had not only apprehen-ded Fred and myself but the two Thai fishermen with whom we had set out for Vietnam all that time ago. Now the Thais appeared in Rach Gia with us. They were the occupants of the other boat discovered a week after ours and referred to in the Radio Vietnam broadcast. I was confronted with them one day in the interrogation room where we all four went to be photographed and rather quaintly measured for new shoes. This was done by asking us to stand on some paper on the ground and tracing round our feet with a pencil. We were to be well-dressed for our first public appearance for six months.

Although we had been promised a release and the prison régime relaxed for a while at this point, I was not entirely at ease all the way to Rach Gia. I had been lulled by false hope before. All the same we were taken to the town in a Dormobile, not a prison wagon, and lodged not in a cell but in a hotel, where I was left free to occupy a small and pleasant room on the third floor without the key being

turned in the lock. Our party met for meals of rice and
vegetables outside on the landing. We were even allowed
a day of rest before the trial and taken out to lunch through
the open streets to a restaurant which might have been
functional by our standards but was a showpiece for top
officials in their country. One of the tables was occupied
by a placard which said 'Reserved UNICEF'. Fred and I
were able to eat on our own at a separate table, which was
quite a luxury. Once again I thought briefly of escaping,
but it would obviously have been foolhardy at this point.
That evening our interpreter came to me in my hotel room
and told me it had been decided that as leader of the
expedition I should speak for the other three at tomorrow's
event. Again we worked on the English text which I would
read in explanation of my presence in Vietnam. Then we
had a little party. The day of the trial was actually Fred's
birthday and he and I and half a dozen of the security
men had a celebration with sweetmeats and coca cola. The
Vietnamese make their own version of this drink which
they put in coca cola bottles left over from pre-'liberation'
days. I found it interesting that the two Thais were not
invited. After the trial they were not taken back to Saigon
with us but remained, probably in our original prison in
Rach Gia in the company of several dozen other Thai fishermen.

In the morning we were taken to the trial. Imagine my
surprise when I discovered it was to take place in the local
cinema, the Cherbourg, a large modern building left over
from French colonial days.

As we walked into the auditorium we had an interesting
surprise. There on the cinemascope screen was my name
in huge green letters, quite the largest I had ever seen it. It
was not projected but painted permanently. I had top
billing too. Richard Charles Knight, I read, and underneath
Frederick Kurt Graham. Over the two names and beneath
were a few lines of Vietnamese in the Roman script they
adopted about two hundred years ago. I asked the
interpreter what the Vietnamese meant. 'The conclusion of
the trial by the Kiang Giang government authorities into
the violation of Vietnamese sovereignty by the aggressors

Richard Charles Knight and Frederick Kurt Graham,' it began, and then it went on to cite one of the interminable laws of the Vietnamese government, 'by order.'

The Vietnamese authorities had even laid on an audience for us; in fact it was pretty well full house, for the cinema was packed with local peasant people plus soldiers and officials, about six hundred of them, all probably as bewildered by the agenda as we were. On the raised stage sat six officials, hard North Vietnamese types bent over papers, and in the orchestra pit was the equipment they had discovered along with us on the island, including the dinghy. On the left of the pit, level with the stalls, four chairs were prepared for Fred, the Thai fishermen and myself. The whole event was covered by local television cameras.

The official at the table started almost immediately. 'Due to the vigilance of the people of Hon Tre Lon,' he began, 'these intruders were apprehended before they could commit any misdemeanour.' He then incited them to applaud, but they were not overenthusiastic. After further speeches, Lee, the English interpreter, indicated it was my turn. He told me to get up and take the microphone, which was to the right of my chair. I was nervous – apart from anything else it had been a long time since I had given any sort of public performance. I accidentally bumped into the microphone, and this seemed to release the tension in the auditorium. The audience laughed just as the children had laughed back in the island hut. I read my statement – it had an illiterate ring from having been worked over in both languages – and Lee translated it into Vietnamese. I wasn't happy with it – it still seemed a devious means of twisting out of me a possible confession that I had been spying – but it seemed the best I could hope for in the circumstances.

It read:

To the Government Authorities of Kiang Giang province I Richard Charles Knight, aged 47, British and an actor, on behalf of the other three apprehended men. I was arrested on the 16th of June on Hon Tre Lon with Mr Graham for violating the territory of the Socialist Republic of Vietnam.

1) I have accepted the conclusion as stated of the investigation

of the Vietnamese Security Department as being right. 2) I would like to thank the Vietnamese Government for the good treatment we have received since we arrived. We have been detained in good condition with good food, drinks, medicine, cigarettes and some reading material. All the interviews with the Security Department have been normal. We have not been illtreated. I thank the authorities and people for their tolerance in view of our misdemeanour that they have kindly agreed to free us all soon. I will try my best to pay the fine. I end by expressing my apologies on behalf of the other three for the violation of your territory and hope that we may receive the favour of the Vietnamese Government Authorities in releasing us as soon as possible. I wish the people of Vietnam peace and happiness.

That was all. I had fought long and hard with Lee, who wanted one final word at the end of my statement. He wanted me to say: 'I wish the people of Vietnam peace and happiness and independence.' I had no intention of my last word to them being political. I was not a political prisoner, as they will know when they read this account. I told him his country was already independent.

We were free but for the money being paid, and that was not free, because there were endless complications. Having established the fine the Vietnamese now thought they would add an amount on top for my food, just as the Thais had in Lancaster's case. This time the Foreign Office won their case and food money was waived. There remained, however, the little matter of £6,000 before I could leave the country, for that was still the shortfall when Fred left on 17 May.

It is ironic that having survived the interrogation of the Vietnamese Fred's now began in earnest, for his bed was moved into my cell a week later when we got back to Saigon. In his euphoria about his release, which he was sure his father would soon secure, he became foolishly anti-Communist and started discussing the Vietnam war in our cell. In all probability our room was not bugged but I felt it was unwise to discuss anti-Communist subjects in circumstances where we were still in their custody.

The other subject which obsessed him was the island on

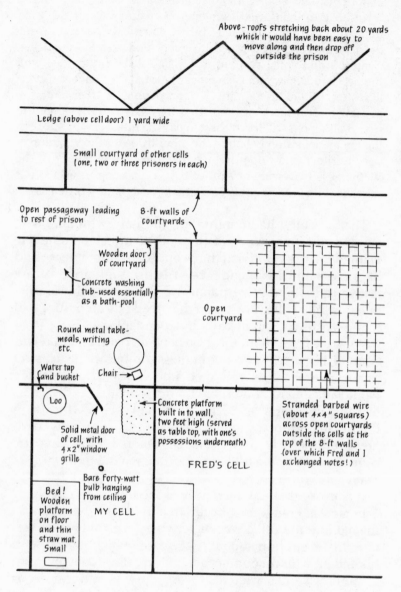

Above - roofs stretching back about 20 yards which it would have been easy to move along and then drop off outside the prison

Ledge (above cell door) 1 yard wide

Small courtyard of other cells (one, two or three prisoners in each)

Open passageway leading to rest of prison

8-ft walls of courtyards

Wooden door of courtyard

Concrete washing tub-used essentially as a bath-pool

Open courtyard

Round metal table- meals, writing etc.

Water tap and bucket

Chair

Loo

Solid metal door of cell, with 4 x 2" window grille

Concrete platform built in to wall, two feet high (served as table top, with one's possessions underneath)

Stranded barbed wire (about 4 x 4" squares) across open courtyards outside the cells at the top of the 8-ft walls (over which Fred and I exchanged notes!)

FRED'S CELL

Bed! Wooden platform on floor and thin straw mat. Small

Bare forty-watt bulb hanging from ceiling

MY CELL

Richard Knight's plan of his second prison in Ho Chi Minh City (Saigon)

which we had been captured. 'What do you really know about the island?' he droned on and on. Again I emphasized that, as much in his interest as mine, I could not tell him more about our mission than he knew already until we were out of Vietnam. He refused to let the matter lie. Every few days he would start trying to winkle information out of me with similar probing questions which led to me shutting up like a clam. Just as I was drifting off to sleep he would wake me with his questioning. At other times he lapsed into complete sullen silence as if to punish my reticence. It was sad, because for the first few days together we had naturally been very pleased to see each other and have some company.

After a couple of months of this we were transferred without warning one evening to another prison in Saigon. It was 21 February 1984. Here we had adjacent cells with the usual rudimentary furniture. The bed was a wooden platform on the floor with a thin straw mat, and there was a wooden chair and a concrete table. There was a water tap and bucket and toilet behind a small partition, and there was one improvement – we both had private yards with a bathtub and metal table out in the open, albeit roofed with barbed wire. Here we occasionally communicated by slipping notes over our adjoining courtyard wall.

One day the guards came to tell him his fine had been paid by his family in America. He was released – and I was given a copy of the works of Shakespeare to read. I got through half of it. To the best of my belief the Thais had long since gone on one of the three-monthly planes that take Thai trespassers back to Bangkok from Ho Chi Minh City. Trespassing into territorial waters as a fisherman is easy enough to do. Up to the very end of my sentence I never quite gave up hope that I might escape. In this prison it was an easier proposition than in the first. I had visions of making a getaway over the low rooftops by dragging myself on to a ledge above the cell door. The tantalizing thing was that I knew the river was only fifty yards from the main prison gate. If I could just get to the water's edge I knew I had a good chance of being able to take one of the local boats, a small sampan, and start making my way to the sea, which was about sixty miles away.

In the event I stuck it out till the guards came for me in August. Till then I was on my own again just as I had been in the very beginning.

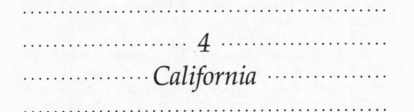

4
California

It had all begun in California five years before. I lived by myself in a hotel room in Santa Monica overlooking the Pacific Ocean. I was the night porter. I was just into my forties and I had had an eventful life on and off the stage. My acting career had taken me all over the world. Sooner or later everyone in my profession dreams of gravitating to Hollywood, and that is just what I did.

I arrived one mid-November day in 1978 via Machu Pichu and Ecuador from Brazil, where amongst other things I had been writing a comedy script which was to be a starring vehicle for my talents. I was determined to show it to a Hollywood producer, so I used my last cruzeiros to buy an airline ticket to the United States. As usual I took advantage of all the possible stop-offs; I am an inveterate sight-seer. But this time I couldn't wait to land in Miami. I was sure I would find the streets paved with gold. I was right, but the gold was not where I thought it was then.

For the first couple of nights it looked as if I had made a terrible mistake. I couldn't afford to leave the airport and slept in the lounge along with the departing travellers. I was plucking up courage to use the telephone number of a fellow called Tom Sutra whom I had met five years previously on a ship called the *Lindblad Explorer* in the Antarctic. Tom lived in Hollywood. I called him and he generously sent me 300 dollars, more than enough for a charter flight to Los Angeles, and for my keep for a while.

When I arrived at LAX international airport near the coast I headed straight for the foothills and the Hollywood area itself, but it was by no means what I expected. It was run-down and seedy, with cheap lodging places, grubby though garish signs, and decrepit people loitering on the streets. Even the palm trees looked dirty. This was surely not the heart of fantasy film land. It was a cold winter there and for two weeks I spent a grim period by myself in a small motel looking for some way to support myself.

One night I found that the 300 dollars had dwindled to just three. I put my bags in a lock-up at Hollywood bus station and walked out into the night. It was bitterly cold and I was regretting leaving my overcoat in Miami airport. This was the place where I thought the sun always shone. That much was patently not true, but I did find the local people very friendly. Again I remembered a telephone number. This time it had been given to me by a girl with whom I had struck up a casual conversation on a Hollywood bus. It was one a.m. by now but I phoned her all the same and she was delighted to hear from me. 'I'll try to fix something,' she said. 'Phone me back in half an hour.' When I did just that she had found me a bed for the night – or rather a floor in a man-friend's flat. He was a most hospitable Jewish fellow who more than lived up to the humanitarian reputation of his race. He invited me to stay until I sorted myself out, and what is more he meant it. He was more generous still and even gave me a little spending money each day. I stayed for three weeks till both he and the girl who had introduced us decided to get married – not to each other but to two other people in a festive double wedding on Christmas Day. It was obvious that I had to leave the flat to the newly-weds and I took up an invitation to join the Sutra family for Christmas lunch.

I was still far from meeting a Hollywood producer. I hadn't even begun to do the rounds of theatrical agents and managers. I discovered Hollywood was a town where ambitions easily fall on deaf ears. Many people have them and few succeed. I picked up a little work here and a little work there, but none of it was acting. Somehow everything I got into seemed to end up like a scene from a comedy sketch. The first might easily have been part of a tragedy, as it happened. I was staying downtown in the cheap mission houses at the time the Skid Row Slasher made his appearance on the Hollywood scene. This dangerous individual behaved exactly as his name implies. He struck on a weekly basis and any derelicts, unfortunates or misfits who had failed to get inside the mission houses by the time they shut for the night at seven p.m. and dossed down on the pavements instead were apt to wake up with their throats cut. Eventually, after three months and thirteen victims, the Slasher was caught, but the atmosphere in the mission houses was thick with suspicion meanwhile. Most of the inhabitants were down and out, derelicts, drifters and tramps. No one knew where anyone came from or where they were going, or what piece of folly, dream or nightmare had led them to this place. It was difficult not to imagine the Slasher was one of the other inmates, the man you shared your room, double-bunked bed or bathroom with.

A break came for me when I was able to fix up a job waiting on tables in the business district of town at a Mexican restaurant because I could speak a little Spanish. Unfortunately I couldn't write it. I was taking orders verbally and occasionally I managed to give the wrong ones to the chef. When two customers got a garbled version of their meal I was sacked. The job had lasted all of three days. The same was true of my next job. This time the dismissal was truly a piece of farce. I was waiting in a newly opened French restaurant with up-market pretensions. One evening a party of six arrived in a celebratory mood. The women were dressed to the nines in gowns both backless and strapless. One of the first duties of any American waiter is to bring to the table automatically before he is asked a glass of iced water for every guest. You can guess what happened. As I arrived with a tray laden with six tumblers of iced water, I tripped and tipped the lot down the back of one of the women. That was the end of that job.

I decided to give up waiting and take up telephone sales. Surely nothing could go wrong at the other end of a telephone line? The Hollywood papers were full of advertisements for jobs offering 500 dollars a week for selling anything and everything by telephone. You are given your script and you take your place in a battery of telephones and are given the phone books of areas all over the United States. I was supposed to be selling office stationery to Chicago. 'Hi there,' I would say. 'May I speak to your personnel in charge of office equipment?' From there it was straight on to first-name terms. 'Hi there, Jane, my name's Richard. How's the weather there in Chicago? You have ten inches of snow? We have a high of 96 degrees.'

It may sound easy, but I was not very adept at the selling business, and pretty soon I joined a telephone answering service. Everyone who is anyone in Hollywood has them to pick up their phones when they are out or otherwise occupied. I sat at a board of maybe two dozen lights with instructions to pick up after the first ring or the seventh ring in the customer's house, whichever way he liked it. Among the clients were politicians and prostitutes as well as film people and I picked up some good gossip, though I had to sign a contract promising not to reveal anything I heard or to make any use of it for at least four years. That's par for the course. I liked this job and after I had done it by day for a while I volunteered to take on nights as well to try to boost the coffers. The trouble was that nobody much bothered to ring anyone else at night. After midnight calls dropped off, and after two a.m. they dwindled to nothing, and only myself and a supervisor were left on duty. One morning at about five a.m. she told me to hold the fort while she went out to pick up a hamburger – you can get food to go at any time of the day or night in Hollywood. She went and I fell asleep immediately. When she returned twenty-five minutes later there were three unanswered call lights flashing on the board. She was furious and I was on the streets again the next day.

It was then that I picked up the job as a desk clerk at the Sovereign Hotel, Santa Monica. It was a comfortable semi-residential hotel where people stayed on a semi-permanent basis anything from a few days to a few years at a time, which meant there were never more than four check-ins or check-outs a week. I did three shifts, three days from eight to four, then two days from four to twelve and one night a week. In return for that I had a room in the basement. I took my script to be copyrighted at the Writers Guild. Bussing up Sunset Boulevard from Santa Monica on the Pacific Ocean, through the wide streets of Beverly Hills, where all the stars lived, I finally began to feel I was in the Hollywood of the movies.

Outside the Guild a young woman was getting into a car. We got to talking and she offered me a lift. As we drove she talked. She was an editor at Samuel Goldwyn studios. When she discovered I was in show business she offered to show me round the studios. She took me into the projection room where a black and white cutting copy of a film was being shown to some shadowy figures in the stalls. She introduced me to them all one by one. Finally she turned and said: 'And this is John.' I realized I was shaking hands with John Travolta, who had just made *Moment by Moment*.

The sun was shining now, it was spring, and the geography of the place was lovely. From the distance the snowy top of Mount Baldy looked down from the slopes of the Sierra Nevada over the flat grid of city streets which stretches for miles and miles and miles and is Los Angeles. As the streets widen out they tumble through eucalyptus groves, through flashy estates where the stucco buildings are hung with bougainvillaea, through hibiscus and oleander hedges straight on to a sandy beach and into the sea. That is where I lived on top of a cliff that I have seen in many movies set in Hollywood. I liked it so well that I allowed my visa to expire. This was lotus-eating in the truest sense of the word. To be honest, there was no way I could get home even if I had wanted to. I earned 100 dollars a week and I spent 100 dollars a week. I drank a little beer, did a little portering and from time to time I wandered over to the city library to borrow as many books as I could carry. One of them was to change my life. It was called *The Money Pit Mystery*.

I have always been interested in unusual stories. I collect them. I was intrigued by the Loch Ness Monster, the Siberian Fireball, Lassiter's Reef. I am interested in the probability of strange events. I like history and one of my weaknesses is gambling. In Los Angeles I used to spend my evenings working out systems of beating the roulette wheel just as I did later in the Vietnamese jail. The difference was that in LA if ever I saved enough from a month's salary I would take the Greyhound Bus to Las Vegas to try my systems out on the tables. But I always seemed to resort in the end to the double-up game of the amateur player where the odds were always 50–50 never 36–1. You put a dollar on red or black, or odds or even, and if you lose you double up and if you win you double up. It is amazing how often a run of six or seven or eight or more comes up on the same choice, but then your luck changes, you lose two hours of hard-earned winnings, and somehow in the end you always come out even. I concluded that I wasn't a real gambler and that I enjoyed Nevada for the glamorous theatrical atmosphere of the place as much as anything. When my luck and my money ran out I turned for amusement back to the books in the library.

I liked stories of treasure as long as I knew they were authentic history. In this regard I had often read about Cocos Island, an inhospitable outpost of Costa Rica where President Roosevelt and the racing driver Sir Malcolm Campbell had both looked for treasure in their time. They were not the only ones. Since 1805 more than 400 expeditions have been mounted to that island in search of three fabulous treasures which are supposed to be located there. Cocos, garrisoned nowadays by three Costa Rican soldiers and a handful of pigs, is the original inspiration for Robert Louis Stevenson's *Treasure Island*.

Four hundred miles off the Coast of Colombia in South America, lies the most romantic island in the world, a tiny speck of land, lonely, uninhabited, set like a green jewel in the blue vastness of the Southern Pacific . . . it rises from the sea, a green mountainous steep, crowned by twin peaks and walled by ramparts of unscalable rock . . .

That is how Campbell described the island. His words exactly pinpoint the romance which is the spur of treasure-seekers. Faraway places, historical mysteries, freelance feats common to another age are at least as important to them as the idea of a lost fortune. Cocos Island has it all. Set miles off the regular shipping routes it holds promise of treasure dating from the sixteenth century to the nineteenth, starting with Pizarro and Eldoradan gold. A band of Incas is said to have landed there fleeing from the Spanish conquistador. They in turn were routed by pirates, who gave their names to the geographical landmarks: Dampier Point, Wafer Bay. Covered in coconut trees, as its name suggests, thick with almost impenetrable tropical vegetation, it is swarming with insects, drenched with rains, crowned with a trio of volcanoes, and lies stifling in humid temperatures of around 115 degrees. There are mysterious messages carved into the cliff-faces. 'Look Y. as you goe for ye I. Coco.' No one has ever been able to decipher them or prove rumours of Spanish gold plundered off Acapulco around 1820 and buried by the English naval officer Bennet Graham, who became the pirate Benito Bonito.

There are more stories of treasure from that period too, of wealthy Spaniards fleeing from Lima, the richest capital in South America, as Simon Bolívar's revolutionary forces advanced in 1821. The Scottish captain of the *Mary Deare* is supposed to have taken the refugees aboard, killed them and buried their fortunes on Cocos. Yet apart from a handful of coins few treasure-seekers have ever come across anything to justify the trip to the island except for the adventure itself. They were often fatally hampered by the terrain, by sharks and octopuses and by the murderous rivalries of other human beings. 'The heat was terrific,' Campbell wrote after his visit in 1926, 'and the bugs bit all the time. Our faces and necks were livid with bites and scratches and the perspiration poured off us until our khaki drill shorts and shirts clung limply to our bodies as wet as though we had just come soaked out of the stream.'

This sort of thing is not everybody's cup of tea and Campbell must have kicked himself a few years later when he realized he had gone well armed with clues but not with equipment. In particular he had not been able to find a metal detector to bring along on his expedition. Then in 1932 a Colonel Leckie and a dowser friend used one only twelve yards from Campbell's shaft. They found a huge hoard of gold, though when the Costa Rican government heard about it they sent soldiers to the island to claim most of it.

41

But to my mind the most interesting discovery was made by one Peter Bergmans, a Belgian who found a two-foot gold madonna in a cave in the Bay of Hope and sold it in New York for 11,000 dollars. The spadework for Bergmans' discovery was done by Captain Tony Mangel, who in 1927 had found some notes in the Nautical and Travellers' Club in Sydney, Australia, made by a friend of Captain Thompson of the *Mary Deare*. He was able to show that all previous expeditions had been looking in the wrong place because they had deciphered the evidence with a modern sextant while Captain Thompson was using a nineteenth-century octant, an inaccurate watch and a compass pointing to the magnetic north. Mangel himself was never successful, got into a lot of scrapes and wrote of 'the curse which pursues seekers of treasure'. All the same, it is his sort of discovery which keeps interest alive.

I knew about *The Money Pit Mystery* from a *Reader's Digest* article that I had idly picked up in a boarding house in Blackpool, where I was doing a season a few years back. I had remembered the title but never bothered to look for the book itself. Those days in Santa Monica I was reading P. G. Wodehouse and James Bond and Sherlock Holmes. I also had a passion for astronomy. All I knew about the Money Pit was that it was the supposed site of an enormous wealth of treasure buried by Captain Kidd. I started to study the extraordinary story more closely.

Kidd was not the only contender for the man behind the pit and I came to the conclusion that he was a pretty improbable one. The theories of what if anything is buried at the bottom of it, and by whom, are endless. Over the years people have advanced the idea that the French, the Spanish, the Incas, the Norsemen, the English, the ancient Egyptians, the British Army, even God himself constructed the pit. In it they variously put the crown jewels of Marie Antoinette, Eldoradan gold, the manuscripts of Francis Bacon proving conclusively that he wrote Shakespeare, and a replica of the Great Pyramid. But for many people the favourite of them all was the archpirate Kidd himself, who was supposed to have deposited a lifetime of spoils ninety feet below sea-level in the North Atlantic.

Over the years since Kidd was hanged for piracy in Wapping in 1701, he has had a bad press. He has been made out by subsequent generations to be a monster, or at the very least a rogue with superhuman powers. As I read, I realized that one of the reasons for this was the belief that he dug the Money Pit, an apparently bottomless shaft in a fairly inhospitable part of the world which would defy even modern engineering to construct, and certainly did to excavate.

The Money Pit is on Oak Island, a small uninhabited kidney-shaped land mass off the coast of Nova Scotia. In 1795 three teenage boys, their heads full of local pirate stories, rowed across from the tiny township of Chester four miles away on the mainland. When they got there they followed an old track and found a ten-foot circular depression on the ground near an oak tree which had had a block and tackle rigged to an overhanging bough. They returned immediately with their fathers and picks and spades and dug down to reveal a man-made shaft with wooden walls scored with pick marks. They managed to dig to ten feet, then they found a wooden platform. Further still they found a layer of heavy flagstones which seemed to have been brought over from Gold River on the mainland. This was obviously man's work and the boys went away to find backers who could bring more sophisticated equipment to bear on the shaft.

Why was the Pit there and what did it contain? After a life's work the boys and their helpers never found out. And despite the involvement of more and more people and more and more investment in the two hundred years since its discovery, no one has ever been able to get to the bottom, literally, of the mystery, because the pit was protected by a system of sluices and hidden flood gates which immediately inundated the pit with seawater at the 90-foot and 150-foot levels, thus protecting whatever might be at the bottom of the Pit.

The reasons for supposing that the Pit contained the vast treasure Kidd was supposed to have taken from the East and West Indies boil down to the following. First, the amazing shaft, when excavated, was found to be crisscrossed every ten feet with solid horizontal platforms made of local wood but also of other materials which had never been native to Canada. The filter gates, too, which let the water through slanting tunnels from the sea, were constructed with exotic materials from warmer climes. Chief among these were coconut fibre and hemp which must clearly have been brought a great distance from the Caribbean regions where Kidd is known to have sailed.

To bring up such quantities of building materials must have been a prodigious effort involving two or three ships sailing backwards and forwards from, in all probability, the Bahamas. It was a masterful piece of engineering which would have called for months of surveys and planning before the builders could embark on sinking a pit in any one of the natural cavities or sink-holes in the area around Mahone Bay. The actual construction would have involved twenty to thirty men working for many months. Kidd, as a well-connected agent of the British government, had the resources and he was the sort of person who had something significant enough to go to such lengths to hide.

Then there was the date factor. Grand piracy and treasure trove had been more or less dead in the Atlantic for almost a hundred years when the pit was found. It was likely therefore that any pit concealing wealth would have been dug before or during Kidd's time, and there were people in Kidd's favourite Caribbean waters, notably the Buccaneers of Tortuga, who had a tradition of constructing such things. Thirdly there was the testimony of Kidd himself. Before he died at Wapping he wrote to the Speaker of the House of Commons: 'In my proceedings to the Indies I have lodged goods and treasure to the value of one hundred thousand pounds, which I desire the government may have the benefit of . . .' He went on to make an offer to the British government whereby he would be kept prisoner on board a ship bound for the site of the treasure and he would reveal to them where it was hidden.

The government suspected a bluff designed to stay execution and did not take up the offer. But pirate-fanciers ever since have thought Kidd did have something to tell them. About seventy-five years after the first casual discovery of the pit, legend has it that a specially formed syndicate brought up from the depths of the earth a flat stone covered with letters and figures said to read 'Ten feet below two million pounds'. That figure and the amount of money poured into the shaft by greedy speculators, who dug down to over 200 feet, earned it the name of the Money Pit. Many people have thought that only Kidd could have had access to that amount of money and that there is sufficient circumstantial evidence to link him with the Nova Scotia area.

By the time he was forty-five, which is the first we really hear of him, Kidd was ostensibly living a decent life in New York with his wife Sarah, Sarah Oort as she was before their marriage. Rather appropriately they lived on Wall Street in the heart of the financial district of Manhattan, and the house actually remained standing till quite recently. Kidd had married late and by the time of the wedding in 1689 Sarah had already conveniently outlived two rich husbands. Kidd became William Kidd, gentleman, no idle description in those early colonial days. In the letters of King Charles II he was mentioned as 'my good and faithful servant'. Yet he may have got up to all manner of unsavoury things, for there was plenty of opportunity in those days for free enterprise away from home. Certainly his crew, many of whom had formerly been pirates, had not altogether changed their ways, for some time after the wedding they seized his ship and sailed her north, leaving him ashore on the island of Maria Galante in the Caribbean. Kidd was then given another ship, and it seems he sailed after them. He was certainly in the north when he took part in the 1694 expedition led by the Governor of Massachusetts Bay against the French in Nova Scotia, which was known at the time as Arcadia.

All this and more I discovered much later on, for when I got back to my room that day in Santa Monica I opened *The Money Pit Mystery* with no more than idle curiosity. As the title suggests, its author, Rupert Furneaux, writing in 1972, is more interested in the pit itself than in Captain Kidd, but I discovered between its pages some interesting speculations. Since the earlier excavations of the Money Pit

some avid collectors of Kidd memorabilia had turned up
four charts from different sources, all reputedly drawn by
Kidd's own hand and all depicting an island bearing an
uncanny resemblance to Oak Island, so called because of
its thick growth of oak trees, quite unlike any of the 360
other islands in Mahone Bay. The charts were collected
together in the 1930s by a retired lawyer living in
Eastbourne, Hubert Palmer. Another lawyer and retired
naval captain, Anthony Howlett, spent a considerable time
researching Kidd and the Palmer collection some thirty
years ago. He published an excellent account of the discovery of the Kidd maps in a now defunct publication
called *Wide World Magazine* which came out monthly in the
1950s.

Hubert Palmer and his brother Guy found one chart in a
chest belonging to the family of Nelson's Captain Hardy
and another belonging to a seafaring family called Morgan
whose ancestor had been jailer at Newgate, where Kidd
was imprisoned for months before his death. Legend had
it that the Hardy chest was cursed by Kidd himself the
night before his execution, when he gave it to his bo'sun
Ned Ward, whose grandson subsequently sold it to Captain Thomas Masterman Hardy. Kidd said that if ever the
chest was broken open his ghost would rise up and haunt
its violator. Carved on the lid of the chest was the skull and
crossbones and the date 1669.

No such rumours attached to the two other charts, one
of which was found in London and the other in Jersey. But
all the charts bore a marked resemblance to each other, and
all had their writing, ink and parchment verified by the
former Superintendent of the Map Room at the British
Museum as the genuine seventeenth-century article. (Since
then the Museum deny their confirmation, but such con-
flicts only served to heighten my curiosity.) According to
Furneaux, the charts were also compared with known sam-
ples of Kidd's handwriting in the London Public Record
Office and seemed to come from the same hand. Three of
the charts were secreted in oak chests of one sort or
another, in false bottoms, or lids; the other was in a bureau.

The clue which pointed to the island off Nova Scotia,

according to Furneaux, lay in the word oak – not in English but in French, which was the language of the original settlers of Oak Island: *chêne*. According to the Kidd charts his island was located in the China Sea. For China read Chene. QED. Furneaux thought that the stretch of water labelled China Sea on Kidd's chart might refer obliquely to the strait between mainland Canada and Oak Island. He cited other facts and fancies, including the way Oak Island was at exactly the opposite point round the globe from what most people understand by the China Sea.

It all seemed a trifle contrived to me, but supporters of the Kidd on Oak Island theory could be encouraged by the geographical similarities between the island on all four Kidd charts and the real Oak Island. There were groups of rocks in the north-west where a lagoon had once existed, and a deep cove in the north-eastern shore which Kidd calls Smugglers' Cove. This gave Furneaux pause for thought. Would Kidd, drawing a map in the middle years of the seventeenth century – for he surely had no time to supervise the digging of the Money Pit in his better-documented latter years – have known the term 'smuggler', a word which came into popular usage in the eighteenth century when heavy customs duties were imposed to pay for Marlborough's wars in Spain? Furneaux checked with the Customs and Excise office and learned that the term was in use earlier in the American colonies, where illegal imports and exports were prohibited by a succession of British Navigation Acts from 1647 onwards.

The circumstantial evidence was mounting to link Kidd with the pit. On the southern shore of his island Kidd has a spot marked 'anchorage' which coincides with the place in Smith's Cove on Oak Island where the local lads, including John Smith, landed in 1795 and found a boulder with a ring-bolt for anchoring boats. Kidd's wrecks coincide with Oak Island wrecks, Kidd's mysterious circular markings with the site of Money Pit, Kidd's other markings accurately suggest the position of some of the engineering works found on Oak Island and built to flood the pit.

Furneaux, stopped in his tracks by Kidd's description of turtles on the south-eastern beach, consulted a Canadian naturalists' magazine and discovered that hardshells and leatherbacks make their way north after July in pursuit of the jellyfish on which they feed. So far so good, but Furneaux himself goes on to discredit the Kidd theory.

Like him I thought Kidd on Oak Island seemed nothing but a bunch of coincidences. It was enough to make me take a closer look at the charts which were Furneaux's piece of new evidence in the 300-year-old story. I started analysing them as calmly as I had started reading the book in the first place, and the germ of an idea lodged in my mind. Kidd's ghost had obviously haunted Hubert Palmer once he found that first chart. It had haunted Furneaux, and now it was beginning to haunt me, as was the idea of his treasure. I imagined he had managed to accumulate his own wealth in the undocumented early years before his marriage in New York when he decided to go straight. He could have roamed the world in forty-five years, starting very young as a cabin boy in the British Navy, and there would have been nothing unusual in that. If Kidd's treasure had not been found at the bottom of the Money Pit – and it had not, despite multiple expeditions with magnificent resources – where was it?

At that moment an idea struck me of such simplicity that it would not go away. Supposing Kidd meant what he said when he wrote on the charts 'China Sea'.

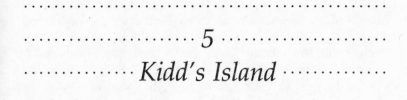
Rupert Furneaux, who wrote *The Money Pit Mystery*, had the story of the discovery of Kidd's charts from Anthony Howlett. He told how Hubert Palmer and his brother Guy had built up a magnificent collection of seafaring memorabilia by the time they retired to Eastbourne in the 1920s. They were both wealthy bachelors, and this is how they preferred to spend their time and their money. They had relics of Francis Drake and Lord Nelson; but Hubert Palmer, in particular, was interested in piracy. He had collected one of the finest libraries in the country on the subject and established a museum devoted to it.

In 1929 he purchased from a London collector a heavy seventeenth-century oak bureau bearing a worn brass plate inscribed with the words 'Captain William Kidd. Adventure Galley, 1669.' The *Adventure Galley* was the name of one of Kidd's ships.

Palmer examined the piece of furniture minutely for secret compartments and indeed found three, though none held anything of interest. Then one day when he was using the table to do his own writing he leaned too heavily on the lid and broke off one of the supporting runners. He then saw that the inner end of this runner had been sealed with wax and an anchor insignia. Inside the runner he found a narrow brass tube with a small piece of yellowing parchment rolled tightly round it. On the parchment was a simple map of an island with the words 'China Sea', the initials W.K. and the date 1669. That was all and for the time being it revealed nothing.

Then, towards the end of 1931, Palmer bought the old chest with the curse on it from Miss Pamela Hardy of the family of Nelson's Captain Hardy. Palmer was undeterred by the idea of a curse and decided to take the base of the

49

chest to pieces. He found that it had a false bottom and secreted in it was a slim volume which contained a sermon. 'Carolus Redux or a Sermon Preach'd on May 29, 1662 being the Anniversary Day of His Majesties Return. By Daniel Cudmore, Minister at Tiverton in Devon. London. Printed for R. Royston, Bookseller to the King's Majesty, 1662' was printed on the title page. Beyond the date it had no particular interest, but the false bottom also contained a map which was almost identical to the first Palmer had found. When he subjected it to scientific tests it turned out to be the genuine seventeenth-century article just like the first. The snag was that it added no further information about Kidd's island. Apart from the words China Sea Palmer had no idea where it was, what it could be called, and there was no mention of any longitude or latitude.

Palmer kept turning up discoveries. The next was a chest which belonged to a Captain Dan Morgan of Bristol who claimed descent from the famous buccaneer Sir Henry Morgan. This was a very unusual find. The chest was well-made, with ornamental brass hinges, and bore a worn brass plate with the monogram 'K' and the skull and crossbones. Inside there was a plaster skull fixed to a plaster model of the Bible. Palmer was delighted. He had heard that such things were used in the swearing in of pirates but he had never seen one before.

This chest had no false bottom but it did have a small mirror set into the lid in grooves concealed by beading. Palmer removed this and found a rectangle of green cloth behind it concealing a shallow well which contained another parchment. This time it was another hand-drawn map of the same island, but there was a difference. The third chart showed the geographical features of the island: hills, woods and valleys, coral reefs, rocks and a lagoon. Then across the chart in red ink was a zig-zag line with two crosses indicating the hiding places of two caches on the island. At the bottom of the parchment were handwritten notes of compass bearings. This was proof that Captain Kidd's treasure, a legend for three centuries, really did exist. Palmer had the chart dated like the others and began to look for another clue: the one that would tell him where

in the world this island was and what was its name. He
advertised all over the world for Kidd memorabilia without
giving any reason for his interest.

In 1934 a small workbox turned up. It was believed to
have belonged to Mrs Kidd and it was now the property of
a retired naval officer living in Jersey. He had inherited it
from his brother who had lived in the United States. This
box was beautifully made, bound and decorated in seventeenth-century fashion, and bore a brass plate on the lid
with the words 'William and Sarah Kidd, their box',
engraved upon it. Palmer bought the box and again he
found a secret cavity behind some beading in the base. At
first he thought it was empty but then he found another
piece of parchment stuck to the bottom. It was another
chart of the same island and this time there was the key
which he had been searching for.

This was a much more detailed chart, with coves and
points named, wrecks indicated and an anchorage marked.
There was also an inscription in the margin giving further
details of where the treasure was buried. On this chart
latitude and longitude were marked.

Hubert and Guy Palmer never lived to find the treasure
or for that matter the island. They tried to solve its identity
and plan an expedition but before they got anywhere the
war intervened. Three years later Guy died, followed in
the late forties by Hubert. Their collection was sold and
dispersed; Palmer left the charts to an Eastbourne friend
who locked them in his solicitor's safe. Pestered by treasure-seekers to the point where he had to have police protec-
tion, the friend sold the charts. But before they were sold
Howlett managed to gain access to them and verify all that
the Palmer brothers had claimed. Howlett had them investigated even more thoroughly than the Palmers. He examined them under infra-red and ultraviolet light and
submitted them to cartographers, to handwriting experts
and to the British Museum.

Howlett was quite a cautious fellow and he still didn't
quite believe the evidence he had. He kept turning up
more, including a sea shanty which goes like this:

51

Eyeless and hairless,
On the island of Pristarius
Kidd's angels do lie.
They guard the death valley,
Through whose narrow alley
Thee'st pass to the treasure
Buried near fathom five.

He looked at Kidd's history from all angles and asked himself every question including 'Did Kidd have any treasure to bury?' In the Public Record Office he turned up a list of the deposits turned over to the British government from caches in the New World at his arrest: two hundred bars of gold and silver, bags containing hundreds of diamonds, rubies, amethysts and uncut stones; more than a thousand ounces of gold dust, two and a half thousand of loose silver; a large chest of silver plate and forty bales of fine oriental silks and muslins. But that was around 1700. Where had he been in 1669, the date on the charts? Where was the island of Pristarius?

Palmer believed he had stumbled on the secret with the aid of a friend called Captain Harold Orchard who had a wide experience of the China Seas and claimed to have landed on an island which fitted the bill. But Palmer's notes on this were stolen or lost after his death. Howlett started again from scratch and though he said he thought he had identified the island he wasn't telling where it was. That wasn't good enough and the story which had died with Palmer and Orchard sounded equally unconvincing to me. So did the story of Oak Island. These people had worked backwards from the island to the charts and convinced themselves that the compass bearings given by Kidd fitted their theory. I would do it the proper way round.

I decided to simply accept Kidd's maps, the direction, compass bearings and all other details as being correct at their face value. If he had written China Sea, I decided to assume he meant China Sea, not some obscure reference to the word for oak in another language. I would decipher the bearings and try to locate the island.

I turned immediately to the map described as the Kidd-

Palmer chart, found in 'William and Sarah Kidd, their box'. This is the one with the inscription round the margin in Kidd's own handwriting. I turned the words over in my mind while I was working, idling and sleeping throughout the next two weeks until I was sure I knew what it meant. Kidd's handwriting is difficult to read in the margin, though clear enough on the map itself when he is printing. This is how I deciphered it – eventually:

360 yards Veer Right North 3 stumps =
55 feet from centre of triangle in Left Rocks
20 feet East of Skeleton of hieb[? or lieb?]

Only the last word was totally incomprehensible to me and was to remain so.

There were other imponderables too. From what point, for instance, was the 360 yards to be taken? From the anchorage, from Smugglers' Cove or from the strange triangle near the wreck at the north-west tip of the island? I knew nothing about the island, including how large it was. It could be 100 miles long or 100 yards, and obviously the size of my task depended on its size.

At this stage it began to look quite daunting. There just weren't enough clues, and if there were, surely someone else had been on to them already. The chart was published in a book for all to see, and anyway the original had been around since the seventeenth century if it was genuine. I began to feel very discouraged. There was a precise geographical position on the map which meant anyone with rudimentary knowledge of map-reading could decipher it if such a thing were humanly possible.

Or could they? On closer inspection the longitude figure is ambiguous. It could be 31 degrees east or 131 degrees east. My interest picked up again. I had enough of a bearing on the treasure itself to start looking for it in earnest if I could find an island. A week later I returned to the library and decided to look up the latitude and longitudes – both of them – of the island on Kidd's chart in an atlas. Latitude 9.16°N, longitude 31°E is in the Sudan. Not an island in sight. Latitude 9.16°N, longitude 131°E is 200 miles off the coast of the Philippines in the Pacific Ocean. Ditto. No islands for miles around. All I had to go on was my hunch about the China Sea.

Still Kidd's ghost would not let me go. I decided to ignore the latitude and longitude figures and spend the spring looking at as many maps of that area of the world as possible. I visited the Marine Navigation Supply Shop at Long Beach and found a few charts of South East Asia. In the main the Americans were only well-stocked with maps of their own coastline. From the charts I found there I decided the most likely place for Kidd's island was one of the Spratly Islands, which were later to be the scene of a grisly massacre of Vietnamese boat people. There was one snag: none of the Spratly Islands was the right shape.

Kidd's intentions were not so transparent as I imagined. All the same I decided to write to the British Admiralty in Somerset, England, requesting copies of old navigational charts of the seventeenth century. I would take a good look at the world as it was when Kidd was familiar with it. I had my answer three weeks later. The Hydrophic Office wrote to say that Admiralty charts were not kept until the year 1800.

It took me another week to make the major breakthrough. I think it happened in my sleep. I sat bolt upright one night and thought that if Kidd had written the charts himself he had done so between 1650 and 1700. That was at least a century before the first charts were kept. It was now nearly three centuries since his rotting corpse had been left hanging for two months for all to see at Tilbury Docks. The world had surely changed a great deal since then, when much of it was still waiting to be explored and all of it was waiting to be accurately documented. One of the things which might well have changed was its way of recording its discoveries. Kidd would be looking at the maps with a seventeenth-century eye. Was it possible that such concepts as latitude and longitude had changed since Kidd's day?

My first reaction was probably not. After all navigation was one of the first of the sciences known to the ancients. They were sailing and discovering mathematical laws and putting the two together when we were in woad. But one thought kept nagging me – they didn't write it all down. No charts till 1800, the Admiralty had said. I decided to look firsthand at what they *had* written down and paid the first of many visits to the University of Southern California Library. UCLA has a superb collection of old and rare books which have to be signed for and read under supervision on the premises of the Department of Special Collections. There I referred to several ancient atlases covering the sixteenth to the eighteenth centuries. They were quite extraordinary, very beautiful, very large and handpainted, adorned with legends in the most ornate script.

But the most extraordinary thing about them was the revelation that, whereas latitude had remained more or less constant in the 300 years since Kidd was hanged, there was a considerable variation in longitude. When he died in 1701 the Royal Observatory in Greenwich on the 0 meridian was only twenty-five years old. If he made the charts as a young man it was probably not in existence at all. Furneaux skates round my conclusion in his book without ever actually coming to it. Howlett mentions possible inaccuracies in the seventeenth century in latitude, which was determined by 'noon sight', a meridian altitude of the sun, and especially in longitude before the invention of the marine chronometer, but he doesn't come up with any formula. Before the observatory was built no one recorded longitude with reference to the Greenwich meridian. If they recorded it at all they did so east of the island of Ferro, the most westerly point of the Azores.

I'll give you just one example of how things have changed over the centuries. I discovered that in 1606 the longitude of Borneo was 150 degrees east. Consultation of a 1718 atlas has it at 130 degrees east. By 1792 it had changed to 120 degrees east. Today it is 110 degrees east. Having said that, it didn't make my task any easier. If Kidd's island existed I realized it could be as far as 2,000 miles west of the position marked on his charts.

At UCLA I threw myself in at the deep end, reading the longitude in the two ways I saw possible. Between 1600 and 1700 the position 9.18°N, 31.30°E would have been in Nigeria, where there were not too many islands. 9.18°N,

131.30°E, on the other hand, was anywhere between
Burma and the Philippines. Now we were getting somewhere. Kidd's island could be anywhere in a horizontal
strip of over 1,000 miles. Again I went back to UCLA.
Every day I took six charts out of the library covering an
area of about 500 square miles from the coast of Malaysia
northwards and eastwards. I examined every strip of coastline, sometimes only twenty miles long, on each navigation
chart, looking closely at each island to see if it might fit
Kidd's island in shape. Allowing a margin of error on the
latitude figure of 9.18°N, I covered every strip of coastline
of Malaysia, Thailand, Cambodia, Vietnam, China, Borneo
and the Philippines between 5 and 15 degrees north, as
well as the numerous islands in the China Sea. Nothing.
By now it was becoming an obsession to find Kidd's island.
But I kept drawing a blank. There were any number of
crescent-shaped islands but they were always in the wrong
orientation or the latitude was wrong.

Every evening when the library closed I would wander
down to a café about one hundred yards away, have a
coffee at one of the open-air tables outside and reflect on
my absurd situation. I was looking at outdated maps for a
non-existent island, a figment possibly of my own imagination or of the imagination of some impostor who had
forged the Kidd charts. Who knew whether Kidd's treasure
even existed? No one even knew whether the charge of
piracy which stuck in 1701 was just or not. The other
charge, murder, was proven. He was seen to hit a rating
over the head with an oak bucket, causing injuries from
which he died. But piracy?

I now started to read as much as I could about the man
whose ghost had entered into me. I imagined myself back
in the seventeenth century. When Kidd was arrested in
1699 in Boston a relatively small amount of money compared to the promise of the Money Pit, £14,000, was
unearthed on Gardiner's Island, New York. Kidd had supposedly taken it from pirate ships in the Indian Ocean
which he was meant to be clearing of their scourge for the
British government. The trouble was he had not brought

the money into port as the law required. What were the reasons for this oversight?

Before the proliferation of modern communications the temptation to secrete some of the spoils of those dangerous voyages around the world must have been enormous. Even though nothing much is known about Kidd's early life and career, if he followed the normal naval pattern of those times he had little to thank the authorities for. He would have joined the Navy or been pressganged at the age of thirteen and worked himself up painfully to superior officer. The pattern whereby freelance spirits improved on these circumstances was also well established. There were pirates who like gypsies lived in communities in the Caribbean and in the South China Sea, and there were also reputedly larger ships which passed in the night and buried huge treasure for the rainy day when they might come back that way and need it.

I knew too that pirate treasure had been found. An English explorer, Frederick Mitchell Hedges, had discovered five chests on the island of Roatan in the Gulf of Honduras which were supposed to have belonged to Sir Henry Morgan. They had found some of Blackbeard's treasure too in Northern Carolina, and Kidd himself was supposed to have a cache in the Caribbean.

From my reading I realized there was no proof whatsoever that Kidd had constructed the Money Pit. Now I began to think the pit had actually not been started until after his death. Around 1763 there was a spate of sightings of fires and strong lights on Oak Island. Several families who had settled near the town of Chester witnessed them but none of them dared investigate because the area was known for pirates. When it was finally discovered in 1790 a block and tackle hanging above the pit were still intact. I thought these might have survived thirty years, but hardly the one hundred since Kidd was operational. The Money Pit was a red herring which had confused Kidd historians too long. A lot of people had exhausted their resources looking for that, and I was probably not the first to direct my attention to the South China Sea.

I had now worked my way through most of the Special

Collections and Navy Charts Department of UCLA with
no luck and was beginning to think there was a reason
why everyone else had ignored Kidd's apparently obvious
message to posterity. Even if his treasure existed he was
not giving the secret up so easily. Still he had given me an
idea for treasure of my own. The next Sunday, 10 June
1979, the following advertisement appeared in the commercial section of the *New York Times*:

TREASURE – Captain Kidd. Authentic copy of Kidd's own map
of his island – send 3.50 dollars and S.A.E. to Suite 210, 3010.
Sta. Monica Bvd. Sta. Monica C A 90404.

This, I felt sure, would make me rich. The Americans
loved the idea of treasure and history and surely could not
resist sending the price of a hamburger for the chance of
pitting their own wits against Kidd's riddle – or merely
hanging it on the den wall. With the money that rolled in
I would run off as many copies as necessary of William
Kidd's chart; the rest would be mine. I thought that would
be at least 50,000 dollars, judging by the circulation of the
Sunday *New York Times*. That was about three million. If
just five per cent of those readers turned to the commercial
pages and read my advertisement and if just five per cent
of those who saw it were haunted by the Kidd ghost as I
had been, I would have my 50,000 dollars. I waited for the
letters to arrive. Within a week, I imagined, I would have
received between 1,000 and 2,000 letters, or 5,000 dollars
in hard cash.

Two weeks later I had not received one single reply, and
I counted myself fortunate indeed for I had been given an
altogether better break. I was right at the point of giving
up all hope of finding Kidd's real-life island when the hard-
working library assistant in the Navigation Department at
UCLA produced a final half-dozen charts. I would spend
one last morning consulting them and if nothing came to
light I was determined that would be that. My passion for
Kidd's island was getting out of hand.

I consulted the first charts and it was the same old story.
No island. Then I came to French Admiralty Hydrographic
Chart No. 3686, dated 1870. In fact I had referred to it once

previously but quite unaccountably passed over what I was to see now. My eyes ran over the groups of islands comparing them to the shape on Kidd's chart. They settled on the largest island of the group. It was kidney-shaped. It was in the right orientation. It had the same two hills marked on the Number 1 Kidd chart. It had the same north-south axis. It had the right longitude and latitude to an incredible degree. It had to be it. THE ISLAND. I was looking at Kidd's own hiding-place. Even the name provided a clue which it seemed impossible for anyone to overlook: Grand Pirate Island. In Vietnamese it was called Hon Tre Lon. It had to be Kidd's island. I was ecstatic. I jumped to my feet and called out: 'I've found it . . . I've found Kidd's island' into the silence of the library.

That night I reflected on my luck. If only one hundred *New York Times* readers had realized the significance of the map I was prepared to send them and only a dozen of those had accurately located its position on the map, as they might well have done, mine would be an altogether different story. As it was, I alone had found Hon Tre Lon, Grand Pirate Island. It was not one hundred miles long but more like a mile and a half, not an insuperable size to explore from end to end, even if my interpretation of Kidd's legend was not accurate.

There was only one complication to getting up and going there immediately. Hon Tre Lon lay in Communist territory.

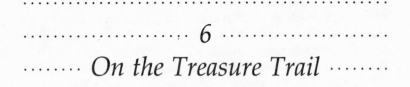
Sooner or later I keep going back to Brazil, which I love. I take a flat in Copacabana and pick up some private teaching jobs giving English lessons to students and businessmen. I have even landed a few turns in cabaret. I wasn't landing any acting jobs in Hollywood; I had not even met my producer. My mind began to turn to Rio.

In the six weeks since I had discovered the secret of Captain Kidd's maps I had already made tentative inquiries about an expedition to Hon Tre Lon starting from Santa Monica, where there is no shortage of yachts or the money to run them. There was even a guest at the hotel where I worked, Robert Radar, a lawyer, who showed some enthusiasm about backing an expedition for treasure trove.

Although Hon Tre Lon lay in Communist territory, to me the problem lay first and foremost in mounting an expedition all those miles away. I would need backers and perhaps companions who were familiar with that part of the world. I found that to the Americans the major problem was a political one. Most Americans found it difficult to contemplate Vietnam rationally given the proximity of the disastrous Vietnam war. Not only that but they also saw the Iron Curtain as a tangible obstruction.

Radar had a plan to sidestep these difficulties. He knew an Englishman living on board a 35-foot yacht in one of the nearby marinas. Since I had never owned a boat I had not really envisaged the challenge of Kidd's treasure in practical terms. This man first indicated to me the extent of the task that lay ahead before I even landed on the island itself. Not only did Hon Tre Lon lie half the way around the world across the Pacific Ocean, it was surrounded, according to the navigation charts of the area, by shallow water which would seriously hamper any boat big enough to make the voyage from Santa Monica. Between the Kidd charts and the modern maps I now built up a pretty good picture of the island in situ and the difficulties in reaching it. As its name suggests, it is the largest of the Pirate Islands twelve miles out from the Vietnamese coast, and for the most part it lay on a sort of continental shelf in no more than two fathoms of water.

I realized I was going to have to take a long hard look at the maps and get professional advice. I was going to need money. I could just about scrape together 350 dollars but that was not going to move mountains or dig for treasure trove. It was August 1979. Everyone who was anyone who could back an expedition for treasure in California was on holiday till Labor Day. Besides my visa was already six months overdue. I decided to use the money to fly to Rio. Perhaps my Brazilian connections could help me get to Grand Pirate Island, which was now my avowed goal. But first I had to get out of the United States. In view of the probable hassle and likely fine at immigration, I went down to San Diego, waited for the last 'shuttle bus' taking Mexican workers back to Tijuana, took the chance of it not being stopped – and went past the control point clean as a whistle.

I continued through Mexico overland at first. As usual I spun out the journey, stopping briefly in Mexico City. There was nothing for me there. Once again Rio did not disappoint me. Before I went to California I had spent three years there and made the sort of friends who might well be able to provide backing for an expedition of this nature. Certainly they would be agog with interest. One person I knew was Ronnie Biggs, the great train robber. I met him first on Christmas Day 1974. The sun was shining, the beer was good and all was well with the world as I sat in my apartment in Copacabana overlooking the beach. Suddenly there was a knock on the door and an Englishman I knew who also lived in Copacabana came bowling into the apartment. 'What are you doing for lunch?' he said. 'Nothing much,' I said. 'Do you want to share my salad?'

My English friend said he knew of a party where we were both invited. Biggs was one of the guests. He was lionized that day, I remember, and since it was the first time most of the people there had met him everyone wanted to know what he had done with the train money. He told an interesting story, describing in detail where every penny of his £140,000 share had gone. In particular, I remember he said that £20,000 was given to a 'lawyer' to invest; some months later, when Biggs was in Australia, he received a telegram from the lawyer: 'Regret No. 20 Smith Street has moved to No. 1'. He was most indignant about it, saying, 'The guy stole twenty grand from me!'

I would not have associated with Ronnie Biggs in a business venture, and he himself would not have had the funds, but this did not hamper our relationship as two Brits abroad. Biggs lived not far from me in Copacabana and after that we started to call round on each other. He always had a couple of girls and several beers in the fridge and he was always good company.

When I was not carousing with Biggs I took in private pupils to pay the rent. Anyone who can afford private lessons has to have a bit of money in Brazil. I thought a couple of them might be interested in providing backing for my Kidd venture. One, a bank manager, couldn't believe his ears when his English teacher started talking about buried treasure. I think to begin with he thought it was part of the course and that the copy of *The Money Pit Mystery* which I had purloined from Santa Monica Public Library was his new set book. He was even more astonished when I brought out the photocopies I had made of the naval charts back there in UCLA Library. But he wasn't hooked.

Much as I enjoyed Brazil, its climate, its beaches and its exotic and easy life, where you can get anything you want, even Brazilian nationality papers, on the black market, it started to weigh on me that I was not getting anywhere near Hon Tre Lon. Each time I nipped over the Paraguay border to renew my visa I knew I ought to be moving on. Apart from a letter I had written to the Vietnamese Embassy in Canada inquiring about visiting their country I had done nothing practical about my expedition at all. It seemed that tourists could visit specific beauty spots in Vietnam as long as they were in possession of prolific documentation, issued as the result of all the usual bureaucratic check-ups. As a man who rarely seemed to find himself with the right visa anywhere, that sort of thing never appealed to me. But even if I could prove myself an acceptable tourist I doubted that Hon Tre Lon would be on the package tour route. I'd have to make a run for it from a more hospitable country.

My route from Rio to Australia took me via Auckland, where I spent a couple of weeks trying to interest an impresario friend in financing an expedition. But first it took me to Tahiti, where Marlon Brando lives. There in the middle of the Pacific Ocean I found myself dwelling on suitable boats for my venture. I took a day trip to one of the cluster of islands, Moorea, on the little inter-island steamer and wondered whether such a thing plied between the Pirate Islands of the China Sea.

Even if there was a steamer in Vietnam, I realized my presence on it as a westerner would probably be impossible, but just as we were coming in to port I saw something which set my imagination going – a speedboat. That had the sort of shallow draught which could cruise right up to the beach on Hon Tre Lon. It also had the speed needed to get in and out without being apprehended. That night, as my steamer returned to Papeete, the Tahitian capital on the main island, it was quickly overtaken by the same speedboat. I realized that a speedboat also has surprising range and stamina. I started to see a way I could make my base on this side of the Iron Curtain in order to get to the island inside Communist territory. It was a good start.

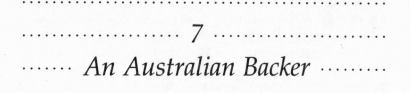
An Australian Backer

In September 1980 I landed from Auckland in the warm summer sun of a Sydney afternoon. I was now 5,000 miles as the crow flies from Captain Kidd's Treasure Island. For me it was going to be a longer route. Still I felt that if anyone could help me achieve my dream I would find that person in Australia. The Australians are sometimes a brash and outgoing people, but it is still a pioneer land full of adventurous spirits and I had met some of them on my first visit there ten years earlier.

In those days I was entertainments officer on a Russian cruise ship called the *Shota Rustaveli*. The ship was named after a Russian poet and its whole personnel including interpreters came from behind the Iron Curtain. But the passengers were largely English-speaking, and the Charter Travel Company employed a fifteen-strong entertainment corps, which was where I fitted in. The package the company offered was cheap, which meant there were a lot of young people aboard, British and New Zealanders and Australians returning home. It was a lively crowd and I soon found out when we docked in Sydney that the cheap fun area of town was Potts Point in the King's Cross area, the Soho of Sydney.

This time I arrived just as I had arrived in Hollywood, footloose and with no job, money or place to live. That's my kind of life. Things happen to you that way. I am not keen on organized holidays or predictable hotels and I prefer to arrive in a place and book into the most interesting accommodation in town I can find according to my budget. I took a taxi straight to Potts Point. The first thing to do was to find a place to sleep the night. This time I soon found a travellers' hostel, where I shared a dormitory with four young backpackers who were seeing the world. It cost only four dollars a night. Even at that rate, money, if you are spending it, does not last long. The second thing to do was to find a source of income, any source, any income. Just as in Santa Monica, which Sydney somewhat resembles, and which also has a large British community, I looked in newspapers and on the noticeboards of shops. I tried the local hotels. Then I got a job as a dishwasher in a French restaurant. It lasted a week. It was a small place and though I liked the French and had married a French girl I just couldn't hit it off with the French owner. I was no nearer to my goal.

At first this did not bother me. Sydney is a wonderfully relaxed place, full of beautiful parks and bays. I could see boats all around and every day I speculated on the sort of craft I would finally choose to get to my Vietnamese island. I lived the typical life of a divorced man – went to bars, picked up girls, went to the cinema. It was a pleasant time and I felt as though I could afford it because I had a wonderful secret which was going to change my life completely. I was in no hurry for change; after all the secret had been kept for three hundred years already. During this time I sometimes wondered whether riches would really make a difference to my happiness. I have said before that I liked my life-style. I had a vague dream of settling down in the sun in a beautiful villa somewhere in Europe, perhaps northern Italy, which I had discovered during my marriage ten years previously. In those days the Americans still had bases in Europe, and though I was living in Paris I was driven from time to time with other cabaret artistes to Verona and other Italian cities by an American Army driver so I could take part in a weekend show there. This went on for about four months when we were not putting on a show at the French bases. A villa in the sun became my dream, but others have had that dream, have had the money to fulfil it and found it did not cure their wanderlust. No, the thing that spurred me on at this time was not the material reward but the unique knowledge that I had unravelled Kidd's secret. I found a job as a waiter and then as hall porter at the New Chevron Hotel in King's Cross. Now I could move into a bedsitter nearby and start looking for a likely backer. I like working in hotels. People come and go, you get talking and usually you get tips.

It was in a hotel that I met Duncan Parrish. We were not exactly introduced but we were drawn to each other over a pint although we obviously came from very different backgrounds. At first I had no idea that Duncan was rich. He was well-dressed in a casual, Australian sort of way. He seemed quiet and sincere and he played his cards very close to his chest. Later I learned that he had two separate luxurious apartments in the countryside and a taste for fast cars. But in other ways his life-style was modest. He was not a roisterer or a big drinker. He was divorced, like me, he had no family responsibilities, and his time was his own. Most of our meetings took place in his office or in hotels. Sometimes we would go to an Italian restaurant for a glass of wine. He did not eat. He was not more than thirty and completely self-made, though what exactly his business was was not entirely apparent. He was a man who liked to keep secrets, and I formed the impression that some of them were quite unusual. But he had an innocent enough ambition of his own. He wanted to buy horses and retire to Southern Australia where no one would be able to get at him. I could sense he was that unusual person, a wealthy man who still had an inquiring mind and was young enough to pursue its whims. He wasn't just interested in making money. He was also interested in spending it – on me and my project.

Of course I did not tell him everything at once. It came out gradually. I met him about three or four times and after a couple of weeks I tried him out on the subject of buried treasure. The best people have the worst reactions to the subject. City types in immaculate pinstripes are inevitably highly enthusiastic the moment they hear of gold pieces – until it comes to taking a chance and outlaying a considerable sum of money which they fear to lose. Then there are as many pirates in the business world as on the high seas. But Duncan Parrish was different. He was the sort of man I felt I could trust. He liked anonymity, he did not like newspaper reporters. I knew he could keep a secret because he had his own. And mine was worth 30-40 per cent of the treasure to him – that was to be our deal. First we would pay for the expenses of the expedition out of the cache, including a cut of 8 per cent each for each man participating in the expedition should it come to a sea trip, then we would divide the rest equally.

It was a good sign that he never probed too deeply as to the whereabouts of the cache I hoped to find, nor the exact nature of it. Though I was reading constantly on this subject I kept the details to myself. My potential backer was astute enough to know it didn't much matter what exactly Kidd had buried on the island. Everything would be marketable in terms of a historic find even if it had little intrinsic value. He was as much caught up in the excitement of how to get at it. The expedition did not really take shape until our conversations began in November 1980. Together we worked out that it would cost up to 10,000 dollars. In fact it ultimately went to around 20,000 dollars. We had such a strong mutual affinity that we had no need to put our names to a contract or work out any rigid formula; besides which no contract for an illegal expedition would be valid. He never set a limit to my expenses, although he was a shrewd businessman and there was no question of an airy-fairy carte blanche deal. Whenever I needed to spend money in those early days I just explained what it was for and he simply signed a cheque.

After my experience in Santa Monica when the English boatowner had gone over the map with a fine toothcomb and emphasized the shallow water, the first thing I decided to do was to take as close a look at the island from as many modern sources as possible. In California the Vietnam war had hindered me. Now I decided to turn it to good use. I knew the Americans must have had a very good idea what the country looked like in which they were fighting, and of all people they would probably have aerial photographs. Now I wrote to the Department of the Interior in Sioux Falls, South Dakota, saying I was a writer who wanted some high-definition photographs of the islands off the coast of Vietnam. They replied saying they themselves did not keep aerial photographs of non-US areas but directed me to both the Director of the Defense Intelligence Agency in Washington, DC, and NASA headquarters in the same city.

This time I decided to save time and contact them by telephone from the Sydney offices of one of Duncan Parrish's suspect companies. It took about twenty minutes to pin down in their computer what pictures NASA had. I told them the latitude and longitude which interested me and they told me they had two satellite photographs of the area, one in black and white dated 1962, the other in colour dated 1965. I was told they would be dispatched on receipt of a cheque from me. When I actually received the photographs they were a bit disappointing from the practical point of view. The colour picture was a glorious, large laminated thing but the island itself was only about the size of a thumbnail on it. Still it meant that the island was a modern reality, not just something in an outdated atlas. This was extraordinarily reassuring and brought it much closer. It was interesting and might at some point be useful. It was now a question of deciding on a definite approach. Legal or illegal?

The idea of writing directly to the Vietnamese government requesting permission to look for treasure on one of their islands seemed out of the question. If they did not directly quash the idea they would want to have every detail, including copies of Kidd's maps. They would then be in a position to simply refuse permission to us and start searching for the treasure themselves. It was unthinkable. So we worked on the idea of somehow getting permission to get into the area and on to the island on some other pretext but not revealing our real reasons. Once on we could possibly use metal detectors to find out if there really was anything there. If so we could go back to Australia and work out the best way of returning to Vietnam and getting it out. As we would be accompanied by the authorities there would obviously be no possibility of just sailing away with it in the first place.

We decided to make an open approach to the Vietnamese government and ask for permission to prospect the area for mineral rights. Everything would be quite legal and above board, except of course that our geological company was completely invented. I hadn't been idle on my travels. During my time in Rio I got a reference from a geologist which enabled me to look up another professional geologist in Australia. I told him I needed a draft letter, which would seem absolutely genuine to any knowledgeable reader. This sort of thing is probably happening all the time in Australia since for some time now they have been in the grip of their own gold-rush. I told you the Australians were pioneer spirits and game for anything. They are also one of the most advanced countries in the world in the field of mineral exploration. So I didn't have to tell my geologist why we needed this, and he didn't ask, but came up with the letter. Meanwhile I was trying to come up with a suitable name for our company. Nothing seemed right. Then one day I saw my new company's name on the side of a coach in the Sydney streets. Australian and Pacific Coach Tours, it read. I had just to change it to Australian and Pacific Geological and Mining Company. It seemed suitably impressive, we thought. With an apparently authentic application from an apparently authentic company the Vietnamese would immediately give us our permissions. Of course we expected they would make a punitive deal with us in case we struck oil or valuable minerals, but we were not intending even to look. We would find what we wanted and be out of the country before their suspicions were aroused. To get to that point our letter needed to be written on notepaper which looked as impressive as the company's name. Duncan willingly signed a cheque for 200 dollars to print up a ream, the minimum amount we were able to order. In the end we used up all of three pages. The paper looked wonderful and I was rather sad when the company had to be wound up almost immediately. Its name was embossed in big red letters on white at the top with four red playing-card diamonds beneath it in diminishing size.

We used an address which was a box number and a genuine telephone number, but we decided not to use our own names. I invented a fictitious director, practised his signature and preserved a copy carefully in case we needed to sign anything again. Then I rang Mr Hung, the commercial attaché at the Vietnamese Embassy in Canberra, and asked him where the letter should be sent. He gave me an address in Hanoi. The letter was typed. I remember it was Christmas 1980, and it was finally sent on 31 December. We were very excited. We sat back and waited for the permission which would allow us to take four men to Vietnam – two real geologists and two impostors, of whom I would be one. At that point Duncan Parrish was preparing to be the other. From there it would be just a short step to Kidd's treasure.

There was no answer. After six weeks we wrote again. Still the same result. It was frustrating but if I had learned anything in the eighteen months since I had discovered Kidd's secret it was that Rome was not built in a day. I consoled myself with the idea that the mining company might not after all be the perfect blind for our purposes. Far better to invent an archaeological company, which would require rather less initial investment in convincing equipment. An archaeologist's favourite tool is his teaspoon. We would certainly need something more than that, a good strong spade at least, but with all this I was quite certain of one thing. In the seventeenth century Kidd had not had a mechanical digger, which meant we would not need one either.

I did my own research for the archaeological company and spent hours in the local library reading up about genuine sites in this area of Vietnam. By the time I phoned a genuine archaeologist for help with a letter there was very little he could tell me about the place and what there was to find – certainly he had no knowledge of what I knew was there. Archaeologists are notoriously competitive and uncooperative, but we discussed the approach to the correct government department and again we had our apparently authentic letter. Again we printed up some headed stationery – embossed in green this time. Again we received no answer. We decided to make one final 'legitimate' attempt to enter the country, and this time we left it in the hands of a genuine tour operator. The Vietnamese do allow tourism from private groups who apply in

The Australian Pacific Geological and Mining Company

. SYDNEY 2000 N.S.W. AUSTRALIA

December 30, 1980

The Embassy of the Socialist
 Republic of Vietnam
31 Endeavour Street
RED HILL   ACT   2602

Dear Sir

We are a geological research company specializing in all types of geological surveys
for exploration and research purposes - including the search for gas and oil deposits
under marine conditions.

We hereby submit an application to send a small initial exploratory expedition to
the southern coastal area of Vietnam.

Purpose: The objective of this initial investigation would be to find out if
              there was potential for the discovery of economic minerals in the
              area.

Objectives: If suitable targets are found it is proposed that discussions would
              be entered into with yourselves concerning the conditions and terms
              under which further research could be carried out. Such research may
              involve various forms of geological, geophysical and other modern
              survey techniques.

Targets: Our initial target would be to find out if there is any potential
              for discovering economic deposits such as phosphates, mineral sands,
              magnetite, tin or other residual concentrates. The initial area we
              propose to investigate is that between Ca Mau Peninsula and Phu Quoc.

Timing: We would propose to send our initial small team of three or four men
              within the next three months.

Hoping we may have your favourable consideration to this application, as we believe
that it may have considerable interest and potential benefit to the Socialist
Republic of Vietnam.

Yours faithfully

GEORGE P ATWELL
MANAGING DIRECTOR

advance and specify the areas they would like to visit. We submitted the names of half a dozen men who wanted to visit the beautiful islands off the coast of South Vietnam. This time we got a reply but it was not the one wanted. The telex from Vietnam Tourism in Hanoi said: 'Regret . . . the areas you have stipulated in your request are not now permissible to visit . . . only published areas through our approved agency in Australia possible.'

Again we toyed with the first possibility – a direct approach to the Vietnamese government informing them about treasure trove which would be theirs in international law but over which they might be prepared to make a deal. But I was still not hopeful about dealing with a hostile régime and nothing has happened since to make me think I was wrong. True the Russians helped mount the much-publicized expedition to lift the gold from the sunken *Edinburgh* off the bed of the Baltic Sea and the booty was honourably sub-divided. Despite their régimes I do not believe the two peoples or the two problems have much in common. The Russian gold was lost during living memory, in an inhospitable part of the world, it is true, but close to Europe and its television cameras and publicity machine.

I was sure I had found the site of Kidd's cache but to most people I was working on a hunch which a greedy government would be the first to confirm. What gold? I could imagine them saying, having insisted on all details before cooperating with me. After that they could just dig it up. It would be a tragedy to lose all the information buried on the island to people who had not the slightest interest in the European phase of its history.

. . . . *8* . . . .

·· *On the Wrong Side of the Law* ··

. . . .

By June 1981 we knew we had to make the difficult decision to mount the expedition illegally. I had been through it all. When I first made my discovery about the island in America feelings were still raw about any deal which included Vietnam. Australia was the most obvious outpost of civilization before Vietnam where I could make careful preparations for what I had long realized would be a very dangerous trip.

During the long periods of waiting for a reply to our 'legal' approaches, I had spent a lot of time pondering on all the aspects of possible illegal approaches. It was quite obvious that the Vietnamese were roundly opposed to any sort of snooping around their coastline. They were probably not even interested in a commercial deal. I couldn't be sure how they would view the arrival of any westerner there by simulated accident. I didn't speak the language. I hardly look of Asian stock. There could be no infiltrating myself into their area of the South China Seas without arousing their well-founded suspicions. Moreover they would be extremely curious to see an obvious westerner years after the Americans had left.

There was a chance that I would be well-treated or ignored by people who had welcomed the American military. But there was an equal chance that they would be hostile or at least take steps to discover my identity as an intruder. Certainly any patrol boat in the area would be obliged to do this.

There was a small chance that the island itself was uninhabited, but this seemed improbable. Most islands of its size, just about one and a half miles long, in the area can support a small peasant population. I imagined Hon Tre Lon would be no different. We thought up various excuses in the event of capture by the islanders or others. The

details would depend on the situation but basically we
would probably have to say our navigation equipment or
motor had broken down. At one point I delved into the
possibilities of taking carrier pigeons with me to convey
messages good or bad from the island. There would come a
time when I heartily wished for those pigeons. Meanwhile
I studied the map of Hon Tre Lon. I decided it probably
had running water. It had an anchorage on the French
navigational chart. According to the Kidd maps it would
be idyllic, with a sheltered lagoon to the west and turtles
playing on a sandy beach in the south.

The French navigation chart 3686 and Kidd's own maps,
on which the island is only a few inches long, could not tell
me much more than this. There is a marvellously compre-
hensive Sydney State Library, however, where I
researched the geological formation of the area, its
weather, its climate, its agriculture. It was probably a typical tropical island but I badly needed to talk to someone
with firsthand knowledge of the place and its possible
defences. And there were people who had exactly that.

During this time I made a habit of roaming around the
harbour looking for boats which had just returned from
those waters. In both Auckland and Sydney I would choose
a boat, walk up the gangplank and ask to see the captain.
Often I was lucky. Western tankers which had come directly
from the area would be in port for three to four days before
moving on. The crew were always happy to tell me how
close they had been to the Vietnamese mainland and what
the shipping was like in the area. The American skipper of
the *Asia Honesty*, a 10,000-ton tanker which had come from
the Gulf of Thailand, was particularly helpful. Captain
Ronne, a man of about fifty-five or sixty, entertained me
three or four times and always broke open his bottle of
Bourbon while he was about it. I warmed to him and actually told him what I was doing, without going into too
much detail. On a couple of occasions he would discuss
the probable strength of any Vietnamese radar in the area
and he actually turned on the ship's own radar explaining
at length the technical details about its performance and
what type of craft and objects it could pick up, which were

mainly metal. If anyone else asked I would invariably say I was a journalist researching an article about the boat people.

And then there were the boat people themselves. I had met and interviewed some of them already in Auckland. Now I made a tour of the camps in Sydney. There was of course a gigantic language barrier, but there were two people who helped me overcome it and my ignorance of their country's coastal waters, a South Vietnamese naval doctor and his wife who insisted on the strictest anonymity but who were able to give me information about the military and radar and shipping installations. I was particularly excited when I discovered that the doctor actually had personal knowledge of Hon Tre Lon, my island. He had been diving off its coast with other naval personnel, who found it the perfect recreational area.

This was the most exciting news so far. I imagined the man had actually walked on the same turf as Captain Kidd. He might have picnicked right next to the treasure. I was aching with curiosity but I knew I had to be a little careful. I had introduced myself as a writer, not as a treasure-hunter. Regrettably I soon discovered that he had never landed on the island itself. He had been stationed at the naval base at the southern tip of Phu Quoc and it was from there he had gone diving two or three times. He could tell me it was obvious that there were people living on the island. There was one other problem about the information he could give me. He could describe the island as it was before the Communist régime took over, though he was unable to remember much of the details, but he had no idea what use it was put to now. The last time he had seen it was in 1965.

My experiences in the refugee camps all pointed to one thing. Whatever happened to my plans they were likely to go a good deal better if I learned a few words of the Vietnamese language. So began one of the most pleasant occupations of my time in Sydney. The doctor and his wife pointed me towards two Vietnamese sisters who wanted to learn English. It was agreed that I should teach them twice a week on Tuesdays and Thursdays, in return for one and a half hours of Vietnamese lessons. The sisters had

75

already resettled in a suburb of Sydney. They were charming and whenever I arrived they first cooked me an oriental
meal. The arrangement lasted for about five delightful
weeks. It has to be said they learned more English than I
did Vietnamese but I was determined to fasten on certain
essentials. It would be necessary to appear cheery and at
ease to anyone I might encounter on Hon Tre Lon. When
it came down to it I suppose I retained about fifty words.
That, in the opinion of Colonel Blashford Snell of Oper-
ation Raleigh, is enough to get you out of most tricky situations you will encounter in other people's countries.

I now discussed with Duncan, my backer, what essentials in the form of transport and equipment and crew
would be needed to embark on an illegal trip. It was clear
I had to get a lot closer to the island than Sydney, Australia,
and that whatever form of transport I finally used I would
have to start from a country in the Far East. I sat down and
listed the possibilities which seemed to be open to me. I
could fly to Singapore or to Bangkok and be a lot closer to
my objective, but when it came down to it I would still be
separated from my island by a minimum of three hundred
miles of water. I liked the idea of crossing them by plane
because of the speed but there was no commercial airline I
could take right to the spot. Was there a plane I could
charter, perhaps?

Besides logging thousands of miles as a passenger I had
no knowledge of planes. I realized with irony that although
I had served in the Royal Air Force at RAF Stanmore – for
two years when I did National Service in the fifties – in all
that time I had been in a plane once. I gloried in the lowest
possible rank of Leading Aircraftsman, which meant in my
case that I had an office job logging the daily mileage of 200
vehicles at the base. One day I was allowed aboard an RAF
cargo plane doing something called 'circuits and bumps'.
That is when the pilot is practising landing and taking off.
He does a circuit, bumps down and takes off again. I could
have done with a versatile pilot now. The outlying Vietnamese islands were unlikely to be rich in sophisticated air-
ports.

I discovered there was a small airfield on Phu Quoc and

another at Hatien on the mainland used by commercial and
military planes. The possibility of landing on either of them
was not even considered. Apart from anything else they
were miles away from the island area. As far as I knew, the
closer islands didn't even have rudimentary strips and the
terrain was doubtless typically tropical, probably swampy,
sandy and covered in trees. One look at the map of Hon
Tre Lon itself showed me that the south and the north of
the island were covered in trees and thick vegetation, and
though the central part seemed open enough there was no
telling what obstacles might be in the way of a landing.
From west to east moreover ran a high ridge. A conven-
tional plane was out, and really a very risky way of
announcing ourselves to possibly hostile islanders.

A helicopter would have been a possibility and could
deal with this terrain, but a helicopter, with its bulk and
short range, needed a sizeable ship to take it within striking
distance – a ship which would possibly draw attention to
itself, even fifty miles off Vietnamese waters. A seaplane
might have been a solution. There was the anchorage in
the west and obviously many other coves. But again the
range was short. The nearest point of friendly land, the
coast of Thailand, was 300 miles away. The seaplane could
get there and back with extra fuel on board. It would not
necessarily have been detected flying at night, coming in
low and setting down a dinghy and crew three or four miles
off the island. But it would then have to wait for at least
ten hours. I feared it was too risky. The amount of time we
dared let it ride in open water did not give us any leeway
in case of difficulties. In the end the cost and the time factor
ruled both these options out.

These were military-style calculations, and naturally my
thoughts turned to the expertise of the Australian armed
forces and in particular to their Navy. They had a possible
answer to my problem – a submarine. I knew nothing about
the cost, the range, the manning, but there was one person
who did, the commander at the Platypus submarine base
of the Royal Australian Navy in Sydney's Platypus Bay.
Nothing ventured, nothing gained. My pose as a writer
had already elicited help from public relations people in

California and at NASA who had provided me with the satellite photographs, and by this time we had also acquired some excellent black and white aerial photographs from the DIA, on which the island was shown about the same size as on French navigation chart 3686 – roughly four inches long.

In Australia I put the same thing in motion. I rang the base and asked to speak to the PR. I said I was a writer and wanted an interview. I didn't have to provide any credentials. Maybe it is my background as an actor but I can usually seem to infiltrate any situation with enough credibility to suit my purposes. This time I think the naval commander was flattered by the idea of featuring in a personal interview. I wondered what he would say when I came clean. The interview took place in his office on the Sydney waterfront. It was right inside the naval compound, where there was no view of the sea. But inside it was just what you would expect. There was a huge desk and ships in bottles. Executive Lieutenant Commander Tom Everard was in uniform, a good-looking man in his mid-fifties with silver grey hair. He received me very cordially and then I told him the situation. I told him it was confidential. I told him I was looking for treasure.

I need not have worried. He looked momentarily surprised, then when I unfolded my maps he was riveted. He doubted whether a submarine was what I wanted. One look at the charts told him as a naval man once more that there was no adequate depth of water around the island. He confirmed the memories of the Vietnamese naval doctor from the camp, who had been diving in water no more than four to six metres deep up to half a mile out from the coast. A submarine needs at least twice its own depth of water. Mine would have to surface some distance out and would then be as vulnerable as any other craft.

I was never discouraged when ideas were shot down if people could concur on firsthand information like this. Their different sorts of expertise led me nearer to my goal. I could almost see and feel that beautiful shallow water. My island was becoming gradually more friendly. The naval commander ventured that a small submarine, a three- to four-man craft, existed which might suit my purposes. I asked him how one could be obtained. Possibly in Australia, he said, but much more likely in Singapore, where there are such things for hire and much else besides. He was very concerned about the dangers of such an expedition and highly recommended that I should be well armed. He favoured Bren guns. I was very sceptical. I didn't want to turn a treasure hunt into a blood-bath. The area had seen more than its share of unrest in Kidd's piratical times, and now. They still have pirates. I'd met the boat people. I'd heard everything I wanted to hear about the Vietnam war. I really believed the treasure could be taken out without any harm being done to anyone. After all I was probably the only person alive who knew exactly where it was. If I could keep it that way no one else would get in to it before me. I believed that a reputable institution like the Smithsonian or the Paul Getty Museum in California would be interested in its acquisition and in making it available on permanent display to the western public for posterity. I was convinced that only a low-key expedition such as the one we were mounting would succeed in everyone's interests.

Again and again people tried to persuade me to use the dramatic approach. On one occasion in the Mitchell State Library in Sydney I met a major in the Australian Army Commandos. Major Richard Riddle, ex-Royal Australian Army, was then senior librarian at the Mitchell. We were both poring over maps and books. After I had met him three or four times I gave him a hint of what I was doing and he introduced me to another ex-Australian Army major who recommended a full-scale commando raid. I was sufficiently undecided to let him introduce me to his friends, and we met over several drinks in Sydney's Pall Mall-style clubland.

The new major could hardly wait to form a group of ten buddies who had fought in Vietnam and knew the terrain. He had it all organized, the arms, the ammunition, the zapping of every obstructive gook in sight. He could get everything he needed, men and guns, in Sydney within twenty-four hours. I didn't want any of it. I told the same to the naval commander. But he was enthused enough to spend two or three hours poring over the maps and the project before he wished me good luck and sent me on my way regretting he could not accompany me. He asked me to be sure to let him know what happened.

Clearly I had to get to Singapore or Bangkok and when I got there I would have to look around for an ocean-going yacht or vessel to get within striking distance of Hon Tre Lon. It had been obvious for some time that the most practical way to go in was by boat – though at that time no decision had been made as to what kind. Obviously it would have to be something between thirty and fifty feet, be it a yacht, motor-boat, Chinese or oriental junk or fishing boat, to make it across the big stretch of the South China Sea. I would then leave it at anchor in a safe cove and for the home stretch I would switch to a more modest vessel which I could conceal under the undergrowth on the beach of the island itself. If I could avoid the patrol boats, well and good. If not I would have some contingency plans. I would tackle that later. I knew there were uninhabited islands about sixty miles at the most from Hon Tre Lon. Pulo Obi was tiny and about that distance away to the south-east. The Pulo Dama islands were closer, forty-five miles from my goal. I thought I could anchor a fifty-foot yacht there and proceed cautiously in a small vessel. For the time being I contented myself with selecting the master boat's crew.

Apart from cruises as an entertainer I really knew nothing of the sea. I'd been to the Greek islands twice, to Scandinavia and on to Leningrad. I'd been to Australia and back on the Russian ship, but like every passenger I spent more time in the bar than on the bridge. On the 5,000-ton *Lindblad Explorer* I travelled to Argentina – in the galley most of the time. I had applied as entertainer but got a telegram back offering me the job of third kitchen hand. I couldn't resist it because I knew the *Explorer* was going via the Antarctic. I spent most of my time below deck cleaning vegetables, peeling potatoes and washing dishes. I was allowed briefly on top at Christmas, when I volunteered to do a cabaret act, and I visited penguin colonies on land and Scott's Antarctic base. I also visited the modern New Zealand, American and Chilean bases, for it is traditional to invite the fifty or so men from them back for dinner on board a passing liner in return for a good deal of hospitality on land – which was the beginning of my undoing. We even called at the Falkland Islands, which were the completion of it. This was before the war, and frankly the islands hardly seemed worth the Argentines' invading. They looked like barren parts of Scotland, windswept and deserted, with very little entertainment for anyone who was not a sheep farmer. The fact is I got stuck into the bar at the Upland Goose with a couple of islanders who invited me back home to spend the rest of the evening. One thing led to another and I missed the Zodiac back to the ship, and when the *Explorer* sailed the next day I only just made it. The chief steward hauled me in front of the captain, where I gave my notice one minute before he fired me. Three days later I left ship at Ushuaia, at the base of Argentina, and got a free ride on a flight up to Buenos Aires. It was the start of eighteen months in South America, spent mainly in Brazil.

I had travelled around the world a good deal but I knew nothing of the area where I would be heading shortly. The treacherous South China Seas which surround the sheltered bay round Hon Tre Lon are some of the most unpredictable in the world, where typhoons and tidal waves could swamp ocean-going liners and tankers, never mind modest little yachts. Duncan Parrish paid my subscription to the Cruising Yacht Club in Sydney so I could scrounge some weekend cruises and get some practice at the tiller. There was also the Wooloomooloo Dinghy Club. Wooloomooloo is a little bay in the King's Cross area and I found three of my crew at the club, where over several weeks we learned to sail everything from rubber dinghy to Chinese junk. They were aged between twenty-two and thirty-two, strong lads looking for an adventure. One was a student, one worked in a navigation office, one was an all-round sports-mad ski-instructor cum teamaker. The fourth member of the crew had replied to my advertisement in the newspapers, *The Australian* and the *Sydney Morning Herald*.

'Adventurous types wanted for unusual four week expedition', it read.

Seven people answered it. I selected three, but after two interviews two of them chickened out. Fascinating my expedition might be but it was proving too dangerous for most people. The third was an interesting young man. I took to him immediately. From the beginning it was obvious to me that he had Jewish blood, which, after my Los Angeles experience, I found a recommendation. He didn't ask too many questions but he loved the idea of adventure. We used to meet in snugs in the Wooloomooloo pubs (one of my favourites was The Frisco). The first time we met I told him very little and I said it must be in the strictest confidence, for his sake as well as mine. I told him I was mounting an expedition to look for treasure. I told him that it was not in Australia and it involved travelling to dangerous parts. I said we would be going by boat. Then I asked him if he was still interested. He said indeed he was, and I said I would tell him more at our next meeting. The week after we met again in a bar. This time I told him we would be going to an island off the shore of a certain country. He asked me what percentage of the treasure would be his. It was not until our third meeting that I told him the country was Vietnam; on the fourth I showed him the map of the island. Now there was a crew of five, including myself. I had started out with four but the third acquaintance of the lads from the dinghy club was so anxious to come along I was sure he would be useful. In four weeks I had the cast list down. The deal was 8 per cent each for the five of us, while the remaining 60 per cent would be split between myself and Mr Parrish, who was still considering joining us.

All we had to do now was to concentrate on our health and stamina. I exchanged my job as a hotel porter for something more physical. Seven days a week all through that summer I followed an early-morning newspaper round with tough work in a packaging warehouse in Wooloomooloo. I cut down on drinking and took up squash. I swam up and down the beach, setting myself distance tests. I wanted to be sure I could swim for a good hour without tiring. I could put in some other practice too

82

at the beach in those days running up to our trip. After much research and many inquiries around Sydney into the various metal detectors available on the market, I had settled on a 700-dollar Microtech 480.

There are many different ways of detecting metal underground now, unlike Sir Malcolm Campbell's day, and when I was in Sydney I think I went into all of them. The most usual for amateur prospectors is a small detector made of a circular plate at the end of a handle with which the user simply sweeps the ground. It is very popular for beaches, where you might find small lost metal objects like coins and rings, but it only detects to a depth of about twelve to eighteen inches. Mine detectors for military purposes detect to a depth of about two feet.

The Microtech 480 consists of a couple of boxes in which there are a transmitter and a receiver separated by a three-foot arm. A radio signal is sent out by the forward box and if it hits metal it bounces back to the rear receiver. It gives a sound or visual signal to the user. Depending on the size of the metal object it can detect to a depth of as much as fifteen to twenty feet, though it is no good for small objects close to the surface. It is used by telephone companies and town councils for tracing lengths of cable and metal pipes which may be lost, unrecorded or old.

Other more sophisticated metal detectors involve one or two men using apparatus such as a proton procession magnetometer, or a method in which two metal electrodes are stuck in the ground to send back a current to a hand-held grid which divides the area into strips. But I figured I had what I wanted. The Microtech 480 was relatively light and portable, and one man could do the job while another kept look-out. After my swim I would go to a quiet area and learn exactly how it operated. On a couple of occasions the whole team practised with it on a deserted strip of sand dunes. Two of us would bury a mixture of metal objects such as tin cans down to five or six feet while the others stayed out of sight. They then covered the whole area with the detector until they got a reading.

At the end of August I was ready to go to Singapore.

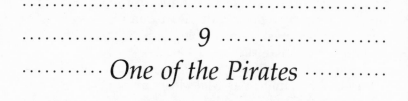

9

One of the Pirates

Faced with the inevitability of an illegal expedition I felt I had to be even more certain I was right about Captain Kidd. I had made my discovery about the island but I had no other documentation to suggest that Kidd had any connection with the South China Seas. I had only my hunch that since the British had been trading there and competing with the Dutch and the Portuguese in an area notorious for piracy he had picked up the habit in his younger days. I had given endless thought to his story and by this time I knew much more than most people about him. In the fine Mitchell State Library in Sydney I filled in the missing link. His story was the story of seventeenth-century England, trying to control a rich colonial trade half round the world in an era of few communications and many rumours. It was utterly fascinating.

Kidd's was the grand era of piracy. It started in the mid-sixteenth century in the western hemisphere when all the European countries were vying for the rich colonial trade in the Americas. It ended suddenly after 1721, when penalties were brought to bear not only on pirates but on anyone trading with them.

In many ways this was the result of the complicated Kidd saga. Piracy ranged in his day from the Barbary Coast off North Africa to the Caribbean and the Indian Ocean and, what interested me now, beyond the Straits of Malacca, north of Singapore. The pirates' names are still familiar: John Ward, Pierre le Grand, Henry Morgan, 'Long Ben' Avery, Blackbeard, 'Calico Jack' Rackham – and William Kidd. There were even a couple of women pirates, Mary Read and Anne Bonny, who had probably started off as prostitutes. Daniel Defoe wrote a verse about them

With pitch and tar their hands were hard
Tho' once like velvet soft.
They weigh'd the anchor, heav'd the lead
And boldly went aloft . . .

There was a lot of literature about pirates, and like everyone else I knew some of it from childhood: *Treasure Island*
inspired by Cocos, *Westward Ho!*, *The Fortunes of Captain
Blood*, *The Pirates of Penzance*, Sir Walter Scott's novel *The
Pirate*, Byron's poem *The Corsair*, and Defoe's *Robinson
Crusoe*, inspired by Alexander Selkirk, a Scotsman who was
marooned by himself for four years on an island off the
coast of Chile.

Pirates go back much earlier than that though. I discovered the word itself comes from the Greek *peiran*, to attack.
By the sixth century BC pirate unions had been formed.
They banded together and governments relied upon them
to fight naval wars for them – they were the mercenaries of
the high seas.

If you crewed a merchant vessel there were many oppor-
tunities to combine trade with plunder, and as long as the
employer got his agreed share not too many questions
would be asked. It was difficult to enforce any law, since
pirates could also be the official navy or merchant navy by
turn. In those days of religious wars and racial prejudice,
states felt justified in taking what belonged to their
enemies, and England behaved just like anyone else in this.
King James I commissioned many plundering expeditions
to the Persian Gulf, and Charles I licensed at least three
ships to roam the Red Sea. When they encountered Mogul
vessels with exotic goods from the Orient on board, they
would bind the crew's fingers together with wire and put
lighted matches between them till they were burnt to the
bone to persuade them to reveal the whereabouts of the
treasure.

There were many priceless cargoes carried in this part of
the world: silks, spices, frankincense, myrrh, gold and silver, ivory, teak, copper and jewels. Most of the pirates
dealt in small stuff and didn't have much of a life. It would
have been marked by gambling, drinking, boredom and

squabbles, with homosexuality and syphilis rife, and terrible violence as they fought for a living. Their enemies too were capable of returning this in kind – a favourite torture of Muslim capturers was the 'instant conversion', a painful method of circumcision.

The pirates got their own back by plundering, raping and killing in the native villages, and they were also quite capable of torturing European passengers who refused to tell them what they wanted to know. I read about one clergyman who refused to speak, who was hung by the wrists from the rigging, had part of his head cut off with a cutlass and was left to die in agony. They pelted their masters with broken bottles and fed them to the sharks in their greed to get their hands on a fortune themselves. Alexander Exquemelin, who was a barber with the buccaneers of Tortuga, wrote: 'some of them will get through a good 3,000 dollars a day and next day not have a shirt to their back . . .' His master used to stand in the street with a butt of wine and shoot anyone who refused to drink with him.

To keep the crew under control captains resorted to some fierce punishments. Flogging and marooning were commonplace for bad language or falling asleep on duty. Ducking from the yard-arm was the punishment for assault, shaving the head and tarring with boiling oil and feathering for stealing, and cutting off a hand for drawing a knife on a senior crew member. But the myth of Treasure Island always kept them going.

An eighteen-month pirate cruise could bring in between £500 and £3,500 per crew member, while a merchant seaman in the same time earned no more than £45. If about one in one hundred got caught it seemed worth it. As late as Nelson's time the Admiral was complaining that 'the conduct of all privateers is, as far as I have seen, so near piracy that I only wonder any civilized nation can allow them.' From time to time then, for appearance' sake, they would crack down on privateers. This nearly happened to Francis Drake, but when the loot captured by the *Golden Hind* was valued – at around £20 million in today's money – Queen Elizabeth decided to keep him on her side.

Captain Kidd was not as lucky. He seems to have been

··

The Plates

··

Copy of the only existing portrait of William Kidd, based on a
sketch made in court by Sir James Thornhill in 1701
(courtesy of Mr R. B. Knight)

Miniature model of *The Prince*, a 1670 man-of-war, in which
William Kidd sailed (courtesy Science Museum, London)

Special navigation course with Capt D. M. Pyett (second right) taken by original team during preparations in Sydney, 1981

1981. Researching seventeenth-century atlases with Major Richard Riddle, ex-Australian Army, who had fought in Vietnam and is now Senior Librarian at Mitchell Library, Sydney

BOCHINH.

Pullo Campello

Kehoa

Quambin
QUAMBIN
TU-N-QUIN

Pullo Ciam
Quenoa

Cochi
QUENA
OTHOA

Kehas
Cazan
Boncheou

Puilo Caam

Cabam
DUTHIOM
Chean ou
Turon

GOLFE DE LA COCHINCHINE

Buiro Is.

Chapia en
de Pullo Scir

Falech

BABOX
GHIA
Cuabia
Ciaxen

Pullo Cam
de la Mer

Pullo Ceci

Felech

Bmdis
QUINHN ou
Nehot Nehot
en Zu dedam
PULLO CAMBI

ROYAUME DE CAMBOYE

Rome de l'Eglise
de Brattaangh
Sombeibus Village
Sombeik Village
Strycmoh Village

Eglise

Loges des
Hollandais

Penompiungh
Village

Terrana

Chantaome
Chantaome R.

Langer

Tarrana

Carol Village

Te Vier

Pollo Way

Pullo Pzuang

Eglise

Balbanont

Assommenum Tour de Surer

Lonchia R.
Buff Isles

PA
ROY: DE
CIAM

Nehot Nehot
Kau Sales

Port
Bengbemar

Iles de
Katuock

Sable de
Middelbourg

GOLFE

DE

SIAM

Pullo Sanceti
Pullo Lornm
Cornae
Pulls Cara

Sandt Grondt, ou
Banc de Rochers

DE LA LE GANGE, où ZIR-BADAD

Pullo Lezin
Patane
Pullo Ridangh

MER DES

Monpracen

des Comados

NAIMA

Matunate

Valcan
BORNEO

Golfe de Romeo

Tanjong Baraun

ROYAUME
DE
BORNEO.

R. de Borulo
Tanjong Stor
Donullana
Laleis

ACCA, ou SORNAU.

ROY: DE
PAHANG, ou
PAAM
PAHANG.

Pentagoram
ou Potangoram

Tangoram

Pullo Capas

Pullo Timaon

Pullo Pesang

Pullo Picos
Pullo
Pullo Tingi
Pullo Tingi
Pullo
Pullo Aoin

Taniong Dato

PARTIE

Sambas

DE

Vieille Sambas
ou omes Sambas
d'omes Laulan
Lonce Naiger

L'ISLE

MALAIE, etc

MALACCA prise par les
Holl. sur les Port. l'An
1641.
MALAIOS.

ESTRECHO DE CINGAP

ANAMBA

Quirimaca

Dalin

Vigia de Sophia
Morro de Buntao

Tanjong Ajy
Boorem

Tameton
Tomahoe

Taniong Mora

ROYAUME

Tanjong Pantour, ou
Pantour

UDIJA, ou ONIAN
JUDIA, ou UPIA Siege Royal
et Ville Capitale du Royaume
de Siam
Dom. des Hollandais
Fort Tlakien
Fortresse de Bankok
Eglise de la
Conception

Bancosoy

Ogme

Kelong

Isles de
Liauta

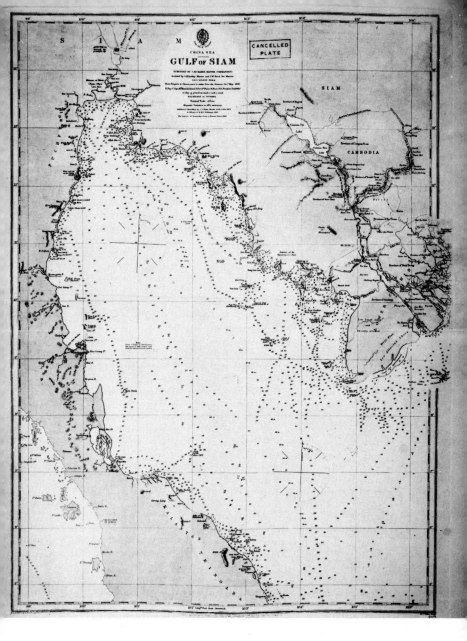

Seventeenth-century map of the South China Seas showing the different latitude/longitude measurements from those of today (by courtesy of The British Library)

Nineteenth-century navigational map of the same area showing changed latitude/longitude measurements (reproduced by permission of the Hydrographer of the Navy)

August 1984.
Arriving
home after my
fourteen-
month prison
sentence in
Vietnam
(by courtesy of
Press
Association
Photos)

made a sort of scapegoat. After all the research I did, I decided he was innocent of most of the charges for which he was hanged. Certainly he made a few enemies in his short life, whether by bad luck or double dealing or both. Even when he hanged his luck was pretty rotten. The first rope broke without him losing consciousness, and he had to be strung up twice. He took it stoically, or perhaps it didn't make much difference to him – the onlookers noticed he was very drunk.

Pirate hangings took place in Wapping in front of huge crowds who would applaud the condemned for their bravado and hold out their hands for the fine clothes they used to wear even to the scaffold to advertise their trade. It was quite rare for people to get as far as the gallows and of all those charged with Kidd, only one other hanged with him.

The piracy for which he paid this ultimate penalty was first reported by two of his ill-assorted crew when he was in the Indian Ocean. He was supposed to be working for the East India Company, the trading arm of the British government in the Orient. In 1697, however, two of his sailors left him at Karwar in India because of his 'ill design of piracy'. They were immediately arrested and sent home to be examined by the Admiralty, on a ship which appears to have also carried a letter from the chief factor of the East India Company at Surat telling the head office what was already common knowledge in the east: that Kidd had gone over to the wrong side of the law.

The East India Company received the letter in August, and on 18 November 1698 they wrote to the Lords Justices accusing Kidd of having seized the *Quedagh Merchant*. It was the start of a huge scandal in which the whole country got involved. Ships had already been fitted out to go to the East Indies and clean up the piracy to which the East India Company was always prey. Commander Warren was put in charge of the mission to 'pursue and seize Kidd if he continue to sail in these parts' and to apprehend the skipper of the *Quedagh Merchant*, a Captain Wright, and ask him why he had surrendered his ship without putting up a fight.

I was to discover that actually Kidd's commission had

been pretty dubious from the outset. He had authority to seize ships with French passes. When he spotted the *Quedagh Merchant* he hoisted French colours to fool Captain Wright, who then allowed Kidd's men to board. Apart from Wright there were three other Europeans on board, two Dutchmen and a Frenchman, and the American owners of the cargo. Kidd asked them if they wanted to buy their cargo back. They offered £3,000. It wasn't enough, so he sent the crew ashore at various ports along the coast selling it off for £10,000. They also allowed Indian merchants to come aboard with goods and then refused to pay for them. Kidd was doing well. He gave the crew £200 each and kept £8,000 for himself and went off to St Mary's Island off the east coast of Madagascar, where he waited for the north-east monsoon to take him back across the Atlantic.

Madagascar was a hive of pirate activity with the best harbour in the Indian Ocean, fertile land and sparkling streams and natives to do the pirates' dirty work for them. Lots of them established quite cosy family lives there and sooner or later they all visited, including Kidd's nemesis, a certain Cornishman named Robert Cullinford. He it was who had been first mate on the *Blessed William*, a privateer commanded by Kidd which had had a bloody battle with the French in the West Indies in 1690. When they had limped into Antigua for repairs Cullinford and the gunner Samuel Burgess persuaded the crew to mutiny and sailed off with the ship while Kidd was ashore getting provisions.

Eight years later in Madagascar, Kidd might well have thought he could get his own back and gain points back home by arresting Cullinford. What happened instead was that many of Kidd's crew deserted to Cullinford with goods from the *Quedagh Merchant*. During this time too, for reasons which remain obscure, his own ship, the *Adventure Galley*, was burned, including its log. Kidd pleaded at his trial that its contents would have exonerated him of any charges of piracy.

First he limped to the West Indies with a new gang of thugs. Rear-Admiral Benbow, who was under orders to sail to that part of the world, was given a circular letter to send to every governor of every American colony telling them to apprehend Kidd should he turn up on their shores. The government also drew up a proclamation offering a free pardon to nearly every other pirate apart from Kidd.

Back home the British public did not know what to believe, but one of their suspicions was that all this had been dreamt up for political gain by enemies of the Lords Justices who had sponsored Kidd's expedition to the Indian Ocean in the first place. Was he perhaps acting under orders from the Lords themselves to go to sea in the *Adventure Galley* and bring back pirated treasure for them? It appeared that even the King was involved, which was not without precedent. London was seething with rumours, which helped make Kidd the most notorious pirate in history and were recounted every other day in the gossip sheets:

[1 August 1699] We have a report that Captain Kidd who some time since turned pyrate in the Adventure Galley and took from the subjects of the Great Mogull and others to the value of £400,000 is taken prisoner by a French ship, the commander of which sent him irons to the Great Mogull.

[3 August 1699] We now have letters from the West Indies which contradict the taking of Captain Kidd the pyrate and say that after the Adventure Galley was sunk he went on board a Portuguese and sailed directly for Darien where the Scots received him and all his riches.

[5 August 1699] Captain Kidd the pyrate, some time since said to be taken by a French man-of-war, afterwards contradicted and that he as gone to Darien, we now hear was at Nassau Island, near New York, and sent for Mr Livingstone one of the council there, to come on board: accordingly he went to him and he proffered £30,000 to give the owners, who first fitted out the Adventure Galley, and £20,000 for his pardon: but 'tis presumed the same will not be accepted.

[17 August 1699] Letters from Curassau [Curacao] say that the famous pyrate Captain Kidd in a ship of 30 guns and 250 men offered the Dutch Governor of St Thomas 45,000 pieces of eight in gold and a great present of goods, if he would protect him for a month, which he refused: but the said pyrate bought afterwards of an English ship provisions to the value of 25,000 crowns and since supplyed with necessaries from other ships.

[22 August 1699] There are letters which say the famous Captain Kidd has surrendered himself to the Lord Bellomont, Governor of New England.

This last was in fact true, and the HMS *Rochester* was ordered from New York to bring him back in irons. The British public, whipped up now by the Tory opposition, were convinced he was a pirate, and they were equally convinced the four Lords Justice were trying to let him get away with it because of their own involvement. Thus when they heard that the *Rochester* hit a storm, was damaged and had to return to port there was an outcry and a public inquiry. I had to sort out the likelihood of what happened after all these years to know whether there was any truth behind the bribe Kidd tried to offer the British government on his way to the gallows, for it is this bribe, or part of it, which might be buried on Hon Tre Lon.

Though nothing is firmly known about Kidd's origins, it is widely believed that he was born the son of a Presbyterian minister in Scotland, in all probability in Greenock around 1645 – the clergyman who administered last rites said he looked about fifty-five. Later I looked up the documents of the trial in the House of Lords, which describe him speaking with a Scottish tongue. He doubtless went to sea at around fourteen in a Glasgow ship, quite possibly in the West Indies trade, and he seems to have been pressed into the Navy in 1673, probably aged twenty-eight. He served in the flagship in the Dutch wars – another pirate, William Dampier (of Dampier's Point on Cocos Island), was on the same ship – and saw some bloody fighting.

Kidd's early feats were rather distinguished. When he was about forty-five he bought his own brigantine, the *Antigue*, and traded with her on the New England coast, marrying his rich widow. He was said to be a very competent commander against the French until his crew mutinied in 1690. Even then he was given another privateer and was so successful he received a special reward of £150 in

1691 from the Governor of New York for capturing a French ship which had terrorized the New England coast. Then things started to go wrong. He was reprimanded for searching English ships from which he requisitioned supplies, and was given no more privateering commissions. He soldiered on, taking a cargo in his own sloop to London where he met an old friend, Colonel Livingstone of New York, who introduced him to Lord Bellomont, the New Governor.

In 1695 in London he drew up the rules for a Pirate Round, financed by the Earl of Bellomont and the four Whig lords to apprehend pirates sailing between New England and Madagascar. Kidd gave a bond of £20,000 and Livingstone put up £10,000 to guarantee his integrity. All goods captured from the pirates were to be accounted for and divided between the Crown and the sponsors and crew of the expedition. The crew were engaged on the principle of no prize, no pay; otherwise they would get no more than one quarter of whatever captured.

This had the makings of a really messy deal, as the public later suspected. They thought the main objective had always been to pirate the pirate wealth and divide it among themselves, particularly since the Round seems to have been inspired by the story of Henry 'Long Ben' Avery, the Plymouth publican's son who had captured the Grand Mogul of India's largest ship, containing, amongst other fabulous wealth, a saddle and a bridle set with rubies designed as a present for the Mogul himself.

For the time being the Round had the stamp of legitimacy. King William III got the customary royal tenth and gave Kidd two commissions. These gave him licence to 'make purchase' of French shipping and to seize pirate ships and their plunder. He was given the *Adventure Galley*. She was a fast-sailer, 250 tons and brand new out of the Castle's Yard, Deptford, in 1695. She had thirty-four guns, a crew of 150 and a distinctive top-gallant sail on her mizzen-mast.

From then on everything seems to have gone wrong for Kidd. He set off from Deptford in April 1696 and refused to dip his colours for a naval sloop. Then a pressgang came aboard and took seventy of his best sailors. On his way across the Atlantic he captured a small French ship and annexed some £900 but gave the crew nothing. He used the money to fit the *Adventure Galley* in New York and took on new crew from a pirate pool run by the ex-Governor Fletcher.

There was one snag to this deal. Kidd had already denounced Fletcher in favour of Bellomont, his protector. Perhaps Fletcher couldn't wait to get his own back; anyway, besides giving Kidd some of the most unreliable cutthroats in the business, he also voiced his doubts about him to the Commissioners of the Board of Trade back home. It was the beginning of his undoing. By this time Kidd had sailed for the Orient, which was of interest to me.

His dealings with the British did not improve. He sighted four warships near the Cape of Good Hope escorting some East India Company ships and boarded the leader, under the command of Captain Warren, to demand new sails for the *Adventure Galley*. Warren refused and Kidd skulked away. Then at Johanna Island near Mozambique he ordered an East India Company ship to run down her Navy pennant, flown by virtue of a commission to capture pirates. He said his commission had precedence. Again they refused to obey him and thought Kidd was acting suspiciously enough to keep their guns trained on him.

He avoided another pressgang but lost a third of his crew from cholera and scurvy. The replacements he took on at Johanna Island were again hardened pirates. He sailed up the African coast to the Red Sea to lie in wait for Indian pilgrim ships returning from Jeddah. At this point he seems to have been flying *le joli rouge*, the red forerunner of the Jolly Roger, signifying that no quarter would be given. The commander of one of the East India Company ships reported a strange red pennant flying from that distinctive mizzen-mast with the top-gallant yard.

While all this was going on Kidd doesn't seem to have had much luck with his haul, which incensed the crew. He tried to take Mogul merchant ships and failed. So far he had only managed to capture that French fishing vessel carrying nothing but salt and fishing tackle. Now he stopped a brigantine called the *Mary*, forced her crew to hand over provisions, several bags of coffee, myrrh, spices, pepper, rice and raisins and £100 in gold. He also took on one of their pilots, who went ashore at Karwar with some deserters. They were the ones who reported him to the East India Company. The *Adventure Galley*, already leaking, was then damaged by Portuguese coastguards off Goa, and the crew were in ugly mood. No one would give him wood or water and he sailed down to Bhatkal, 200 miles north of Calicut, where he took all he needed by force.

Still, however, the great prize escaped him. He let two ships by because they were too well armed. His crew lost patience, and it was now, during a fierce argument, that Kidd hit a gunner over the head with a bucket and killed him. This was one of the charges which stuck at his trial.

He captured the *Thankful* in November and later that month the 200-ton Indian-owned *Maiden*, which was carrying a French pass and so complied with the terms of his contract. He went on to the Laccadive Islands, still off the west coast of India, and did his share of plundering, raping and pillaging the native villages. In January he was in the act of plundering a Portuguese ship when he was driven off by two Dutch vessels.

And then in February 1698 the 400-ton *Quedagh Merchant*, registered at Surat, hove into view off the Malabar Coast of India. Kidd thought the syndicate back home would be delighted. Although she was Indian-owned and had an English captain she had a French pass and was laden with jewels, silks and muslins.

In the library I looked up lists of some of the pirate hauls described by the Admiralty Courts in England in the seventeenth century. The *Cimba* yielded 2,070 pearls (valued at the time at £80), three ounces of pearls, two strings of pearls, three bunches of pearls, two single pearls (£20), two pearls worth twenty gold pieces, garnets set in gold worth £30, a ruby, a polished diamond and fifty silver pomanders. There were brilliant garments too: one kirtle of velvet, one kirtle tufted with taffeta, one lady's toga in silver brocade.

The *St Paul of Malta* yielded 'Muscadells' laden in Venice, a butt of malmsey, twenty quantities of English arras, twenty carpets, bed furnishings of damask, a bed-hanging of crimson and white damask, a bed-hanging of Turkish cloth, bed-hangings striped in gold, taffeta striped in gold, a damascene garment lined with catskin, a striped garment lined with rabbit skin, a taffeta garment lined with squirrel, 120 handkerchiefs, six silk quilts, fifty napkins of linen, four tablets of ebony engraved with the image of Christ, two diamonds, two gold chains, a pair of bracelets, one ruby, a pair of agate beads with paternosters in gold.

Then there was the haul taken by the *Tilbury Hope*: a basin and ewer of silver, twelve silver vessels, three little packets of silver, three cloth packets embroidered, two silver candelabra, eleven silver plates, two silver saucers, two gold bracelets, silver salt cellars, one kirtle of wrought velvet, one crimson damask petticoat and money to the value of £7. That was just from a little Dutch vessel captured in the Thames itself.

Malabar, where Kidd took the *Quedagh Merchant*, is the south-west coast of India. Kidd would have to cross the Bay of Bengal and go through the narrow Straits of Malacca into the Gulf of Thailand to reach the area I was interested in, the South China Seas, well patrolled by pirates. It was a journey of more than two thousand miles. The area was not heavily populated – when Thomas Raffles founded the British settlement in Singapore in 1819 its population amounted to 150 fishermen and pirates, thirty Chinese and 120 Malays. These were used to plundering eastern vessels but on the whole they had learned to leave western shipping alone. There were enough western ships there preying upon each other. Now we were getting somewhere. Whether or not Kidd had time to cruise the area beyond Sumatra himself, I knew from my reading there were western ships which had done exactly that – ships which Kidd himself met up with subsequently.

One was the *Charming Mary*, the other the *Mocha*, captained by Cullinford. They cruised the Malacca Strait north of Singapore, the entrance to the Gulf of Thailand, where Hon Tre Lon was situated, and goodness knows what vessels they might have apprehended there. When they were not there they used to lie in wait together off the southern tip of India at Cape Cormorin. There they took a big Portuguese ship with the Governor of Malacca on board. They got 300,000 rupees and goods and the promise of another 100,000 for the ransom of the Governor.

In 1697 they took a Portuguese ship bound from Goa to Macao. They took another bound for Manila. They intercepted the East India Company's *Dorrill*, carrying twenty guns and bound from Madras to China, at Pulo Berkala off the east coast of Sumatra. In other words there was plenty of interchange of cargoes and vessels from the part of the world which interested me, and Kidd had participated in these exchanges. Perhaps part of his plunder had included the little map I had deciphered. Had he been able to buy his freedom from the British government he could have gone back for this haul and happily lived off it.

The first thing Kidd did when he heard he had been designated a pirate beyond the Act of Grace on his arrival in the West Indies was try to get ashore at St Thomas but he was refused. Then he started running round the Caribbean like a headless chicken.

Off Puerto Rico he found a sloop called the *Antonio* owned by a merchant named Boulton, and the two set sail for the island of Mona between Puerto Rico and San Domingo. Boulton then went to Antigua to bring back provisions on the *Antonio* and on a brigantine belonging to a Mr Burt. They then all anchored in a remote river on Haiti and transferred some of the *Merchant*'s treasure to the sloop and the brigantine. Kidd himself then went north to Long Island on the *Antonio*, leaving twenty men to guard the *Merchant*. Naturally the men sold off the cargo to passing ships, earning themselves £300–400 each.

In Delaware Bay Kidd anchored off Lewiston and landed a seaman called Gillam with a heavy chest. Then he ran up Long Island Sound to Oyster Bay, where he dispatched a letter to a lawyer friend in New York asking him to get in touch with Bellomont on his behalf. This Emmet did and returned with the postmaster of Boston, Duncan Campbell, to persuade Kidd to sail to Boston. In the meantime Kidd had been busy. He had transferred chests and goods into three sloops and put them ashore at Block Island.

Kidd hoped that Bellomont would grant a pardon, and he sent him the French passes to prove he had only acted within orders. But he also sent some things to Lady Bellomont which looked very much like a bribe: an enamelled gilt box with four diamonds set in gold and two rings valued at £60. He gave Duncan Campbell a hundred pieces of eight and some muslin and other goods, and to Mrs Campbell he gave gold chain and further pieces of muslin.

He gave the master of the sloop carrying Campbell to the *Antonio* a bale of white calico, muslin and some sugar and some pieces of Arabian gold to a friend of Campbell's. Then before he went to Boston he went to see his friend John Gardiner on Gardiner's Island, where he landed two bales of goods, a heavy chest containing gold and silver, two or three other chests, two negro boys and a negro girl. He spent several days hovering between Block Island and Gardiner's Island, landing more things. There seemed no end to the goods he was able to distribute. On his way to Boston he landed some more goods at Tarpolin Cove, and when he encountered a Boston sloop he presented the master with a bar of gold asking him to take a bag of pieces of eight to Boston with a Turkey carpet, a clock, a small bundle supposedly containing some clothes for Mrs Kidd, who had come aboard with their children at Block Island.

Kidd's negotiations with Bellomont failed. He offered him £60,000 which was aboard the *Quedagh Merchant* in Haiti and the £14,000 which was recovered from Gardiner's Island. He was clapped in sixteen pounds of irons and sent to a damp jail in New York where he was harangued by the preacher Cotton Mather and then sent to England in 1700 to languish in Newgate Prison before standing trial three times at the Old Bailey. The French passes were never produced, though they did turn up two centuries later in America. Kidd's tarred corpse was hung in chains at Tally Point to deter others from what he was supposed to have done. Even the offer to the Speaker of the House of Commons to lead him to the *Quedagh Merchant* and his treasure,

which he now valued at £100,000, did not sway the outcome.

One thing was certain to me after reading all this. It was
not for lack of money that Kidd hanged. Whether or not he
was innocent was something which entertained the seventeenth century but need not concern me. What was unfor-
givable to them was that his manoeuvres around the
subcontinent, annoying the Grand Mogul of India, had
made things more difficult, not less, for the East India Company.

Poor Kidd: he was turned into the biggest bogeyman
till Blackbeard, a continuing figure of terror in American
folklore. Seamen still fear his ghostly pirate ship with Kidd
brandishing a cutlass aboard. One legend tells of a pirate
spectre, his clothes drenched with water, knocking on
farmhouse doors in New York asking the way to Wall Street
and paying with gold coins from the east.

I had the known facts. I was also sure I had been able to
read Kidd's mind. Ever since he had tried to buy his
freedom with treasure and had been refused, treasure-
hunters have tried to find his loot. They have looked in
New York, Nova Scotia, Florida and Haiti, but no one had
ever looked in the east. Kidd had been there for the East
India Company. Other Europeans had been all the way to
China. That was documented, so either way my theory
held up. I still believed he could have been to the Orient as
a young man too. The British had traded in India and further east since the seventeenth century. There was an
island 100 miles down from the Vietnamese Pirate Islands
where they minted coins. My feeling was that Kidd could
have had his own ship by his mid-twenties and been leader
of a band of pirates. He could have deposited the caches
on Hon Tre Lon in the 1660s before he turned up in New
York.

There are of course other possibilities. He may only have
been a crew member and have assisted in burying the treasure, after which he made the maps of Hon Tre Lon to
remind himself where it was – as was the custom.

It is a popular misconception that pirates, especially the
well-known ones like Kidd, Morgan and Blackbeard, had

an enormous amount of treasure which they kept in one place or carried around with them. The truth is that they would have had several treasure deposits. They might live and operate in one area of the world for a few months or years, accumulate a fair amount of spoils, deposit them in that area and intend to return for them later, drawing up a chart as an aide-memoire meanwhile. They would then move off to a different part of the world, similarly plundering and hiding quantities of goods in some local cache.

By the time a pirate captain was forty years old he would have half a dozen hoards in many different areas. The probability was that either he never returned to collect them, for maybe he was comfortably enough off with what he already had elsewhere, or he was prevented from it by death. Unless Kidd's secret had been discovered in his own lifetime I was confident his booty was still there.

All treasure stories seem to focus on a ship laden with booty captured over several months. A landing party of about half a dozen men is then detailed to row out to an island at dead of night and bury several chests which they intend to dig up a few months later.

I don't think pirates were as naive as that, and certainly they were not good at working in unison. It is much more likely that after plundering a couple of ships on the high seas they would divide the proceeds between captain and crew in the usual 60–40 ratio, and the latter would return to their community and to their families. Or they would put into port and the crew would blow it all in a few days on wine, women and song. The captain would be unlikely to abandon his vessel for long – Kidd had lost his when he left it in the West Indies. He was also unlikely to have much faith in the crew, and whatever ideas he had to conceal his portion of the treasure he wouldn't want to share them with half a dozen cut-throats in a rowing boat. He knew they would just come back at a later date and dig it up for themselves. So he would have done one of two things. He would decide on a small uninhabited spot only he knew on an island or a deserted coastline or in a bay or cave, and he would take the vessel there with the crew and anchor a way off, out of sight of land.

He might have used the place several times already, hence the several caches, like a bank deposit drop or a safe. He would not share his secret with anyone on board. Even if it was a long task he would take the treasure lot by lot to the spot and bury it himself. He would carry the chests, put them in the ground and fill them with treasure. Then he would cover the hole and row back to his ship. Then he would weigh anchor immediately and set sail on a long trip to lessen the chances that any of the crew members would remember where they had been.

There was another method. It was gruesome and quite certainly very popular because it was so convenient. He would take a couple of other men with him to help him do the heavy work and when they had finished he would quite simply kill them. I think Kidd used this method on Hon Tre Lon. I think he went straight afterwards and never went back for the treasure, which was always there for a rainy day. But at the time he had one helper with him and he buried him next to the cache. That is why his map reads '20 feet East of Skeleton of [Mr] hieb [or lieb]'.

I had discovered Hon Tre Lon and Kidd's connections with it. I had no idea exactly what had happened in his days, but it seemed to me that the odds were heavily stacked in favour of there being treasure on the island, and for that matter on other islands which had not been found since the heyday of piracy. I also knew what sort of things would have been buried there to make the trip worthwhile. At the very least I expected to find coins: British, Portuguese gold ones, Chinese and Annamese. I was raring to go.

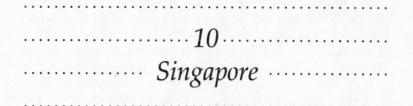

10
Singapore

Singapore looked pretty good when I arrived in early September 1981. Despite my predilection for globetrotting it was the first time I had ever been there. It was warm and sunny as I wandered through the shopping plazas checking out the modern shops and having the odd beer outside on the pavement among the multi-racial crowds.

Although I was still 600 miles from my destination I had decided to go to Singapore to pick up equipment precisely because the shops were so good and stacked with cheap electronic goods. My exit from Australia had been unusual. I was again six months overdue on my visa. Up to about that time New Zealanders did not need a passport to visit Australia, so I switched on a Kiwi accent at the Immigration and said I had been living in Sydney for two years and had no passport. No problem. I flew to Auckland and then Singapore. Duncan had given me an initial float of one thousand dollars, but more was available by banker's draft as and when it became necessary. This time I didn't need to check into a hostel. But I was fair to my backer. The time for luxury expenses would be after we found the treasure. I ignored Raffles, the white wedding-cake hotel of empire, where you could still imagine Somerset Maugham and Noël Coward lifting martini glasses to each other on the balcony – and found a moderately nice hotel with a swimming pool near the centre of town.

Singapore is an island, so I was looking forward to having a choice of boats. How to begin in a country you don't know at all? At first I stayed in my hotel room and used the Yellow Pages. I phoned everyone. I located the marine stores and two major yacht clubs, the Changi Sailing Club and the Republic of Singapore Yacht Club. I visited both clubs. I just walked in. No one asked any questions, so I

100

sat down at the bar, and pretty soon got into conversation. Among the people I met was Captain David Iradell, a bohemian American of the old tradition who had picked up many Vietnamese boat people in the South China Sea. At both yacht clubs my conversations came round to the question, were there any yachts for hire – bare-boat. In Australia, in Santa Monica, in Greece, the answer to this would be 'Which one do you want?'

In Singapore I was surprised to find it was not quite so easy. There is lots of tourism but not quite the proliferation of leisure sports. Owners of prestige boats are the privileged few. Many of them didn't need to rent out their craft, certainly not to a stranger. They were an adventurous bunch too. They wanted to know what the story was, and even though I didn't tell them they wanted to come along.

I said my plan was to visit the Tioman Islands with several friends. The islands are a well-known beauty spot, good for diving and swimming, lazing and fishing, about three days' sail up the coast of Malaysia. What I didn't tell them was that under cover of a trip there and back we intended to cut across the gulf over to Captain Kidd's island. Several boatowners looked interested, so we discussed terms. The price seemed to be between 1,500 and 2,000 dollars for a week to ten days.

I was looking at 45–65-foot boats, but I decided to leave the exact choice to my crew, who were still in Australia. They had much more experience than I did and I had plenty else to do. I rang the UN to get permission to visit the Vietnamese refugee camps in Singapore as I had done in Australia. I also had to check out all the equipment and ammunition stores so that we would be able to get hold of everything we needed in double quick time just as soon as we had settled on a boat. If we could locate one with depth-sounders and life-saving equipment, well and good. If not, we had to be prepared to buy all the necessary extras to ensure the success and safety of our trip. All I had brought with me from Sydney was the metal detector for when I arrived on Kidd's island and a 16-mm camera. The crew would follow with other equipment.

After a week in Singapore I flew on to Thailand, slightly

nearer to my goal. I left Bangkok quite quickly and went on to Pattaya beach where I imagined there would be water sports and yachts for hire. But Thailand proved devoid of yacht clubs. I spent a week moving up and down the coast, travelling as far as Chanthaburi, fifty miles from the Cambodian border. I could go no further because of the military presence; but here, just 200 miles from my objective, I could get a good idea of the sort of weather and temperature to expect in Vietnam. It was hot and cloudy with some rain.

In the atmosphere of secrecy and isolation in which I was living surrounded by the Thais my thoughts began to dwell on the problems of arms and ammunition. By now it was obvious to me that people carried them routinely in the South China Seas, including people who go yachting for pleasure. Just before my arrival in Singapore there was the case of a French couple who were cruising happily in the gulf when they were boarded by the crew of a Thai boat. The wife foolishly went below and reappeared with a gun, and the intruders shot her on sight. Her husband survived the ordeal but the boat was ransacked and cast adrift.

The couple had probably assumed the boat to be an innocent Thai fishing boat when it first approached. This is the guise under which the notorious pirate boats of the gulf operate and have been operating since Kidd's time. These boats don't fly the skull and crossbones, but they might as well. Today they look like any other eastern fishing vessel, about 70–100 foot long, with a speed of ten to twelve knots and a curious grilled superstructure which distinguishes them from other eastern craft. Many of them actually operate as fishing boats, but they are pirates on the side.

In Singapore I had found that access to the refugees who had experience of these pirates was easy, but not information. Not unnaturally the refugees did not like to dwell on the horrors of their passage. After two visits I had met someone who had left Vietnam about six months previously. He came from Saigon and did not know the island area where I was headed, so he could not tell me much about the shipping thereabouts, but he had a heady tale to tell. Despite the need for internal passports he had managed to get to Rach Gia, 100 miles from the Cambodian border, and thence to an island twenty miles south of it. The island was patrolled by guards but he hid in a cave for forty-eight hours. All his plans had been made in advance through a sort of resistance network. At midnight on the second night he picked up a small fishing boat on the coast and rendezvoused with the refugee boat five miles offshore along with refugees from all over Vietnam who had used the same intelligence network. It was a common story. Some of these boats floated around for more than a month getting into trouble because of high seas, engine failure or interference from pirates who knew the refugees would have all their portable valuables with them. One man told me how he was twice stopped by pirates who took two women, raped them and then searched the ship for loot. Other boats got through to safety in three days.

I could get arms in Bangkok easily but not a boat, so I decided to return to Singapore and telephoned Australia to summon the crew. They were raring to go. We all arrived in town on the same day and checked into the same hotel. We spent a couple of days acclimatizing ourselves with a round of drinks and Chinese meals. Then I introduced them to my short-list of yacht owners. Here we hit a difficulty. The Tioman Islands where we were ostensibly heading were generally a bit far south for the rough stuff; all the same the Singapore boatowners had heard about the French couple, and many similar stories were doing the rounds. One Australian, used to the Thai coast and pirates, was sailing his yacht single-handed when he was approached by a Thai boat. He didn't hesitate. He fired two warning shots – which didn't deter the Thais. Then he loosed off, killing several of the crew. There was an inquiry, but he got off on the grounds of self-defence. So the boatowners were as nervous as we were about this sort of thing. For them it might mean losing a £50,000 yacht. Again and again the same thing happened. We could sail the boat for as long as we liked but only if the owner came along.

They made all sorts of excuses. There is a cosy little club run by a French guy on the north shore called the Marina where a lot of Australians and New Zealanders and westerners live on their boats, many going to work each day in the city. To them a couple of thousand dollars for a week's rental is a windfall, and it seemed as if they might be tempted to play along with us. One guy was nearly there when he said it was too much hassle to put his wife and kids in a hotel for a couple of weeks. Then there was a German fellow who was most interested in our plans. We agreed on a price, 1,500 dollars with a 2,000 deposit, and on a departure time – in a week. The yacht was a beauty, with all the latest equipment, including SAT-NAV, a small navigational device which uses a satellite to locate your exact position in the ocean. The crew, who were much more obsessed with sailing than I was, had spent some time in Sydney trying to find one of these; they cost between 3,000 and 5,000 dollars for a medium-sophisticated device which locates your position within two miles. They continued the hunt in Singapore, even though Duncan Parrish back home was not all that keen to contemplate a major optional investment of this kind. The German boat had it built in.

Everything seemed set. Then the skipper said he wanted to come along. The old story. We explained we were all old friends who wanted to be alone together. He said he would think about it overnight. The next day he asked to meet with us in a bar in the Singapore Plaza. After a couple of drinks he drew me on one side and said: 'Can I have a private word with you?' We walked about twenty yards away from the rest of the crew. A hundred things were running through my head but not this one. He said: 'Tell me straight, are you all queer? Are you going off for a sex party?' I assured him we were not, but that even so he couldn't come along. He obviously didn't believe me and thought he was missing out. The next day he said we couldn't have the boat after all.

Then we really seemed to strike lucky. A Californian had an even better boat. It was small, only forty-five feet, but it was compact and outstandingly well equipped with safety gear and depth-sounder. More to the point it had a very good dinghy, which was an essential point of our plan, for we were unlikely to be able to sail up to a Communist island and anchor right off its coast. Our relations with the

Californian were extremely friendly and the crew spent a lot of time with him getting used to the boat, so it was not surprising that one night he asked us all to a party. I had no wish to go. There was no point in getting too close to him because then he would certainly ask questions and we would only offend him if we could not answer. Still three crew members decided to go along.

The next day we all met in my hotel room to spread out the maps, as we had done so many times previously, and discuss our final plans for the trip. This time something was different. No one said anything, but there was a tense silence in the air which made me apprehensive. Two days later, with only four days to departure day, the Californian announced that he had changed his mind about hiring the boat bare-boat. It was a terrible blow and it unleashed a whole string of unforeseen events in its wake which as it happened were for the best. On questioning it appeared that the crew had been drinking too much at the Californian's party and someone had said something indiscreet. They didn't spill the beans completely and reveal the purpose of the trip, but they hinted they had plans to go further offshore than we had confessed. That was too much for the proud boatowner. I was left without a boat and without a crew member too.

On reflection, trouble had been brewing ever since we met up in Singapore. Though we had spent the whole of the previous winter together, learning to sail and to navigate, it is always a difficult thing to get on at really close quarters provided by a boat. Now we were having a dry run. Though I had a hotel room of my own, the other four were sharing two by two. Three of them were pretty close friends, and then there was John, the man who had answered my newspaper advertisement, who was the odd man out. In the end he was to prove most loyal to the expedition, but trouble started between him and the Wooloomooloo member who had tacked himself on to the party at the last minute. He was an immensely experienced sailor, the oldest of our little bunch apart from myself, but he had personality problems. He was unpredictable. I knew it but I thought we could overcome them in the spirit

105

of the expedition. It was not to be and it was a good thing we found it out when we did. I didn't want to be isolated in the China Sea with a maniac. There are three situations in which a man's real character comes out: marriage, in a prison cell, and on a small boat, especially over a long sea trip.

The disagreement blew up over something quite stupid – a taxi fare. Gary thought he had been overcharged, which he probably had. Singapore taxi-drivers are no different from any other taxi-drivers. But Gary became the typical outraged tourist. John, a much more happy-go-lucky Aussie type, told him to calm down and not be such a bloody idiot. But Gary persisted. The difference of opinion refused to go away, and four days later, when we were on the point, as we thought, of clinching the deal with the German, Gary came to me and said he was leaving. I didn't try to stop him. He had come to Singapore on a cheap return. Now he spent his own money on getting back to Sydney. Now we were four.

The indiscipline must have been infectious and probably came from the tension under which we were living, running up hotel bills, unable to stay put, unable to carry on and bound to keep our secret. It is difficult to live at close quarters, particularly when money is tight, which it was sometimes. One evening we got ourselves in quite a fix when funds from Duncan in Sydney had failed to arrive on time. For some days we had been running up our rooms and most of our meals on credit. The manager was very nice about it but he said it could not go on. Then he confiscated our passports. The crew looked to me to get them out of this. While we were drinking in the bar that night I remembered that the same thing had happened to me when I was on my honeymoon in Switzerland. On that occasion I had simply gone to the manager of the largest hotel in the small village in the Jungfrau mountain area where my wife and I were staying and asked him if I could do my cabaret act in his night club. He agreed and gave me a reasonable fee for my performance, which was enough to get us out of our jam. Naturally the crew expected me to do the same in Singapore. I woke the next morning quite resigned to the idea of doing the rounds of all the night clubs. As it happened it wasn't necessary, because the fund arrived that very day.

These things had taken their toll and Gary had already left for Australia by the time the other three decided to go to the Californian's party and let their hair down and tell – just enough to scupper the trip. In the event of all the set-backs, I was not too concerned. We had no boat, so we needed no crew for the time being. Duncan moreover was concerned about the bill we were running up. We decided to disband while I made further inquiries. It was arranged between us all, with Duncan's approval, that the crew would return to Australia and I would move up the east coast of Malaysia to continue looking for the right boat.

I was absolutely confident we would find the right boat and our time together in Singapore had just given us the opportunity to hone our story properly and to give a cred-ible answer whoever asked us. Boatowners were one thing. Patrol boats were another. We were quite aware we were likely to be spotted sailing a luxury yacht in Communist waters. What could we say in our defence? We worked out that we would throw all our cameras and equipment overboard, immobilize the SAT-NAV, say we had drifted into Vietnamese waters, perhaps even invoke their pity over a crew member with a game leg. Either way we would get rid of all trace of any arms we were carrying, or perhaps we would not carry arms at all. I had long come to the conclusion that this was the best solution in the circum-stances, especially if we were sailing a yacht in and out of Singapore. The island state has the most rigid laws on arms carrying and other things. In Malaysia you may incur the death penalty for being in possession of a gun, and in Singapore while I was there a mother of four was hanged for possessing three ounces of cocaine and heroin.

In the end the only thing I bought in Singapore was four cameras – two Kodak instamatics, a cheap Konica and a Super Eight cine with tripod. I had arrived from Sydney with a 16-mm cine camera acquired second-hand, only to have it stolen from me in a Singapore plaza while I was making a telephone call from a public box. It was a bizarre episode. I laid the camera in a shopping bag at my feet and as I was speaking someone tapped me on the shoulder and grinned in my face. I didn't know him and he didn't know me, but his accomplices must have known there was something interesting in my bag. When I looked down it was gone. I replaced it with the Super Eight, packed the metal detector and other equipment which was still intact and got on the bus across the causeway to the Malaysian border. I knew exactly where I was going.

The bus rattled its way up the flat drab landscape of the east coast of Malaysia, broken occasionally by small villages and attractive stretches of palm beaches. There was only one sizeable town on the map – Trengannu, with a population of maybe 20,000 people, a small tourist trade and four hotels. It looked a likely spot, but in the event I got off the bus sixty miles to the south at first and stayed a day looking at fishing boats in the small harbour there. The germ of an idea was entering my mind. By evening it was obvious that there was nothing hireable, so I continued to Trengannu.

I wouldn't call Trengannu a beautiful place. There are two or three main streets with western-type three-storey brick houses, supermarkets and modern shops, a Chinese quarter with ramshackle thatched bungalows which extends along the waterfront full of motorbike shops, and the outlying Malaysian area with its characteristic bamboo huts roofed with folded banana leaves. Beyond that it is open flat country and thickly wooded areas given over to forestry. A wide river bisects the town full of little islands at its mouth which were to become very important during my stay there. Further up river, where the Malays ply up and down to collect timber, there are crocodiles and monkeys. Offshore I think I detected a couple of sharks, or perhaps they were dolphins – I still can't tell the difference when I see their fins streaming through the water. Still the ragged tourist trade has no fears about using the sandy beach. There are no shark scares as in Australia, but then there are no developed leisure industries. There were no water sports and certainly no yachts for hire.

I got off the bus and booked into the Panton Beach Hotel,

the best in town, though these things are relative. For two weeks I just walked around. In towns like this in the Orient there is always someone who knows how to fix everything. In Trengannu it is Mr Awi, a man with four wives whom he kept in four separate houses; he had a small schooner and spoke reasonable English. Mr Awi lived on the largest island in the estuary, which is reached by ferry from the port. After four or five days I was directed to him and told him I was a writer who wanted an unusual holiday. I told him I wanted to hire a boat and live by myself and that money was no object.

Awi said he knew of a thirty-foot boat owned by Mr Abdul. We visited Mr Abdul for tea. This was a very formal occasion, characteristic of how business is done in this part of the world. Mr Abdul's boat resembled a Thai pirate vessel without the superstructure. It was numbered rather than named, as working boats are in this part of the world. He said it would be ready in three days and would cost 600 dollars for a month's hire. I thought this was a high price and 400 dollars was nearer the mark.

All the same I wanted the boat badly. The monsoon was coming up and with it unpredictable weather. I didn't want anything to go wrong this time, I had no need to haggle over money and I was in no mood. I went as far as to pay Abdul on the spot, and two days later I went to see Awi confident that I could board my boat. It had come to this. We were not going in like James Bond in the speedboat I had seen in Tahiti, or in the luxury of a Californian yacht, nor under cover of a submarine. We would chug into Vietnamese waters in a humble fishing vessel, certainly not capable of doing more than ten knots, with no sophisticated navigational aids on board.

Awi had a problem. He explained that Malay fishing boats were part-owned by the government. In this way they subsidized local fishermen, who in turn paid them a percentage of their catch. Having taken his 600 dollars Abdul had gone to the local authorities and mentioned casually that he had rented his boat. The authorities immediately withdrew permission. I shrugged. I was confident there would be other fishing boats. The town lived from fishing. There was another problem, said Awi. Abdul had spent the money. Neither of them seemed to understand that I was entitled to it back. We argued for hours and in the end the money was handed over. That is a typical Malay situation.

The Panton Beach Hotel was costing me forty dollars a night, or rather that was the cost to my backer, who was getting nervous at all this delay. In the security of Sydney, where it is easy to get things done, he couldn't envisage the mentality of the Malays, and I certainly didn't hold this against him. I decided to move to a cheaper hotel, which made my progress even slower. The new hotel was further from the ferry. Now I had to take a rickshaw to the port, wait perhaps an hour to get over to the island, then hope that Awi had come up with something.

It was while I was hanging around the port that I discovered the Honey Saloon. You could certainly get into trouble there if you wanted to, though I had enough trouble on my mind. The saloon was a curious Chinese-Malay institution, a barber's shop cum massage parlour cum bar. The bar was tiny, about ten foot by ten, located upstairs on the first floor. It was really a waiting room for people who wanted a shave or haircut or – something peculiar to Chinese saloons – to have a sort of ear manicure. The assistants would work hours on a man's ears, cleaning them and plucking the hairs. They would also do a very chaste massage – through the clothes. I often volunteered for that, as I was pretty tense at the time. They would massage your arms, your hands, your legs, but not your feet, for some reason.

In the back room I believe there were more intimate sessions by arrangement. But the assistants in the bar and in the shop were very correct and very beautiful in their cheong sams slit to the thighs. I nearly fell seriously in love with one of them, who was about nineteen and exquisite. I visited her often and toyed with the idea of asking her out. She was almost certainly looking for a husband, and this would have suited many men. She came of a good family and there could be no other deal. The Chinese have a great respect for family life which I admire.

Malay society is very restricted, and it is not easy to meet women. In the Muslim quarter many of them are veiled. They are not allowed to leave the house once they are married and have to send their children off to do any errands outside the house. These things are taken seriously, because there is a religious police to enforce the morality. Any assignation is reported and offenders are sometimes beaten with a stick called a rotan and the number of whacks is reported in the newspaper. A single girl meeting a man must be chaperoned, and foreigners dating girls are quite simply thrown out. I didn't need that at this juncture.

All the same my Chinese friend was lovely. She wouldn't need chaperoning because she was not Muslim, but we would have needed an interpreter if we were going to spend an innocent evening together. She didn't speak a word of English. I thought I would take her to a Chinese restaurant. After a couple of evenings we would dispense with the interpreter. There was a chemistry between us, but it was all too complicated, and half reluctantly I decided to concentrate on the problem of the boat.

Awi was still working on the problem and after a while he found a second boat in which the government did not have shares. It was a pretty ramshackle old craft but just about seaworthy with a 33-horsepower motor. We agreed a price; we agreed I could sail it alone. Then he took me on a trip, and the motor broke down. Awi fixed it but it showed itself to be quite unreliable. I was quite relieved because I didn't fancy a 600-mile trip in this unpredictable vessel.

Then a third boat came up. It belonged to some of Awi's neighbours and it was in much better condition. It was a 35-foot fishing boat, about ten years old, but its motor was in good condition. Again we had to go through the time-consuming tea-ceremony while money changed hands, the agreed fee of 600 dollars for one month and a deposit.

The boat was perfect. It had three holds for storing equipment and further space beneath the engine where only the most curious would look. It had a small covered cabin where I could sleep and shelter from the rain with an open back which I covered with plastic sheeting for privacy. In front there was a little wheelhouse. I rang Duncan in Sydney, reversing the charges as usual, and told him about my success. He was delighted. So were my crew – though not all of them, for after Singapore one had disappeared up the Malay peninsula on holiday and lost interest in the expedition. Now we were three.

As a matter of fact I greeted this news with some relief. This boat was even smaller than the yachts we had scoured in Singapore and it would have been difficult to house five grown men and the equipment we needed. Especially difficult if we were all going to get temperamental, and it was difficult to see how we would not in the circumstances. In the event three seemed to be a perfect number. It was also lucky. I told them to be prepared to sail in two weeks' time; meanwhile I would get the boat ready. What happened next was pure farce.

I have spent most of my life in the theatre. I won one of my very first theatrical jobs in a Swanage summer show by doing a Danny Kaye impression. I sang his 'Tchaikovsky' song about fifty Russian composers in thirty seconds. It was in 1955, when he was very popular. Some time in the future I look forward to making comedy films. But the best comedy is to be found in life. At Awi's tea-ceremony I was introduced to the boatowner's sons. This was to be our next problem, for one way and another he always arranged that they should chaperone me.

At first I agreed to take one of the sons with me for a week while I was learning to handle the craft, but just how much apprenticeship do you need to sail a Malay fishing boat? You fill up with oil and petrol, you crank the motor and flick three levers, and it runs for eternity. Sometimes when I arrived in the morning he would be sitting on the boat grinning and pointing to the sea. I indicated in sign language that I wanted to be alone to think and to write. He indicated that the waves were tricky and continued to sit. This way we would meander round the bay smiling at each other happily, neither of us getting any closer to our goal. Mine you know about. His was to find out about mine.

Not surprisingly the Malays just could not understand

113

me. They don't like to do anything alone. They love to gossip, and they can't keep secrets. If ever I managed to avoid the owner's sons and get a good early morning start I became aware of a boat following me. It would laze around a little way off. I would anchor and it would anchor. We would both get out our fishing lines, then I would go back to port and it would go back to port. Still I felt confident they would tire of the novelty of the mad writer in town and leave me alone, so I proceeded to load the boat.

This again was not easy. I had told the Malays I was just going to sail up and down the coast and wanted privacy. Now I had to introduce the idea of a couple of friends with huge appetites. How else could I be seen to be stockpiling huge supplies of food and water for a possible three-week trip at sea. I told Awi a couple of Australians might join me. Not unnaturally they remarked they thought I had wanted to be alone. I looked aggrieved and so did they.

I decided not to arouse the curiosity of the locals too much by bringing bulk supplies on board every day. Like it or not, they were curious, for the boat was moored right in front of the island, either 100 yards out where they sometimes dropped me off – even the ferry was known to make a detour – or at the jetty right in front of the houses. I kept my methods simple. The basic tools of the trade were two plastic carrier bags which I filled with corned beef, cartons of orange drinks, baked beans and processed cheese from the local supermarket. Together with this I took some writing paper.

Every other day I took a trishaw from the hotel, past the port police, got on to the ferry, got off at the island, asked someone to row me out to my boat, spent the day there, left the provisions well-hidden in the holds and returned with the writing paper. I even did a little genuine writing, keeping a journal. Sometimes food was the last thing in the bags. I also had to board the two metal detectors, which looked a bit like portable stereo equipment with collapsible long handles. I wrapped them up in plastic and tied them with string, put them in the bags and hid them under the front deck gaining access through the engine room. No casual visitor would ever find them, only the customs if they were bent on a search, in which case I planned to say I was going to look for coins on a beach and hadn't wanted my valuable equipment stolen. I also had my augers – geological hand-drills which look rather like a three-foot corkscrew. These I wrapped in sacks and similarly concealed. In between I played the friendly, cheerful drinker to one and all.

On the whole I avoided those dimly lit upstairs bars where tourists drank with the local divorcees, who were offering their favours at a price. That was the only living open to a girl who was divorced by her husband, but on the whole she much preferred to ply you with drinks till you passed out and she got a percentage. I had my American-style bar run by a Chinese family which was a cut above most of the joints in Trengannu. You could eat pretty well there. I was never one for de luxe meals but I liked this place on account of one of the sisters who worked there. I think she thought I was quite mad. No one stays any time in Trengannu. I was pretty tense and I used to get a bit drunk before I asked for the menu. There were all the usual things, steak and fish, but I only ever ate one dish – shrimp cocktail. I asked for it by chance during one drinking bout. It was delicious, so I asked for another. I was too drunk to go on to the next course and the pattern was established. I would eat shrimp cocktail after shrimp cocktail. It seemed silly for them to have to prepare them one after another so I usually asked for six shrimp cocktails all at the same time.

Meanwhile the hippies came and went. That's the only sort of visitor who comes to Trengannu. I swam a bit with them on the beach, but I always had to get back to my loading my boat. I tried to make friends with the owner's son. I offered him a cigarette in the hope he would leave me alone. He didn't. I tried to practise making quick getaways. You had to climb down to the engine room beneath the waterline under the cabin, pull back the three levers, crank the motor, flick the levers forward. It required a knack as much as anything.

I got quite good at this, but I wanted an electric starter motor. It was much more prudent to have one for quick getaways if necessary. Since there was a switchbox in the

engine room I realized it must have had one once. I decided
to ask Awi. Whenever I asked him for anything it was
the start of an enormous round of business. Quite simple
things were an opportunity for him to demur, to concur,
to bargain, to fail me and then to come up with the goods.
But it always took at least two days when it should have
taken two hours. It also always seemed to cost me at least
twice the price it should. That is the way business is done,
and who would have said no to it had they had all the time
in the world on holiday. In my case, time was running out.
Not only was the monsoon coming on; I had to keep an
eye on my visa.

I had everything I wanted except the freedom to use the
boat alone – and a dinghy. Though the vessel had changed,
the dinghy was still an essential part of the plan. It had to
be a ten- or twelve-foot dinghy, with motor and oars. It
could be made of rubber, wood, fibreglass, anything but
metal, just as long as it could withstand a ten- to twenty-
mile seatrip fully loaded. We might have to go that far in
order to escape detection. The trouble was there were no
suitable dinghies locally. I toyed with the idea of going back
to Singapore to buy one, but I knew I would be charged a
crippling amount of tax on the border. As it was, all this
dithering around was costing the backer at least thirty dollars a day.

Then Awi's friend delivered the final blow. He wanted
the boat back. It was the end of October. He said I could
have it for another week but no more. Now I had to unload
it, plastic bag by plastic bag. It didn't seem very funny at
the time but to an outsider it must have looked hilarious.
Gradually my hotel room became heaped with equipment.

I started looking for another boat just as the monsoon set
in. This time I had a contact in Chennering, ten miles south
of Trengannu. Chennering was nothing but a modern harbour with a new cement quay and very few facilities. It
sounded unpromising but this time I struck gold. As usual
I met the owner, I had tea with him, I took a few trips up
the river in his company to give him confidence, I gave him
750 dollars a month to be sure to be allowed it bare-boat.

The boat was a medium-blue typical fishing vessel in

relatively good condition. She had the annoying habit of taking on water at anchor when it rained, which it was doing most days, but I knew from experience that was the way these boats were built. If I left her unattended for more than a day I just had to bale her out and that was that. But once I had found her, things moved quickly. I even found a light twelve-foot fibreglass dinghy with a good four-horsepower outboard motor and two oars. My new boat had no name, just like all the boats in that part of the world. Its number was TFA 1396. TFA and I were going to get to know each other quite well.

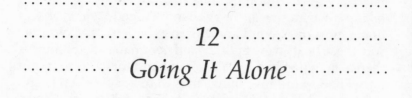

12
Going It Alone

It was now December 1981. It was about 75 degrees outside and we had already lived through the beginning of the monsoon. The unmade side streets were awash with mud. The rain would pour down regularly, but the sea was still fairly calm. Now I had to transport everything from Trengannu. Sometimes I made the journey by bus, sometimes I hitched a lift, sometimes I would take a taxi from Trengannu. I would sleep on board, and in the morning I would wrap up everything I had stowed, hide it and go back to Trengannu. In this way I loaded quite large articles like blown-up inner truck tubes which were to serve as emergency life-rafts. It must have seemed peculiar to the other guests to see a grown man trundling these in and out of his hotel room. On the other hand it was quite reasonable to explain that since I was going on a two-week trip I should make all the proper contingency plans. As it happened no one asked any questions.

The last and biggest problem for the time being was fuel. TFA's tank held about ten gallons. I needed at least 150 to get us to Hon Tre Lon and back. I stocked up with a reasonable amount at the port in Chennering, where they sold diesel fuel on the quay, but the rest obviously had to be taken aboard in secret, otherwise I might arouse too much suspicion and the extent of my plans be revealed.

I evolved a circuitous method of hiring one trishaw in the morning and setting out to buy second-hand jerry-cans each holding 5–7 gallons. I would then deposit these behind a gas station saying I would come back later in the day. I would return after dark, waiting perhaps a full hour for a trishaw to come by, get down the beach and carry the heavy cans 150 yards two at a time to the dinghy, and then to the boat, where I stored some of it in 10–15-gallon red

118

plastic dustbins. Diesel fuel is non-inflammable, so I figured they would be safe from that point of view, but I had
to rope the dustbins in an upright position to keep them
stable at sea. I also had about twenty gallons of fresh water
to bring aboard in jerry-cans.

I was all ready to go when the monsoon started at sea.
The wind whipped up the waves, and it would have been
quite nonsensical to make the trip. Every morning I
mooched half a mile from my hotel to the beach and stared
out at the inhospitable sea. The weather was quite unpredictable. Once a week I phoned the weather centre in Kuala
Lumpur to ask for their forecast all the way up the gulf. As
soon as there seemed to be a break in the sea conditions I
would telephone my backer in Australia and tell him to have
the crew ready to come out at a moment's notice. Then two
days later the weather would break again and I would have
to put them off. This did nothing for the morale of the two
remaining members. One of them was quickly running out
of funds, and soon he had to get a job. Now we were down
to two, John and me.

Towards the end of December I phoned my backer, Duncan, and asked him to tell John to be ready within seventy-
two hours. Still the sea was rough. By now John had my
telephone number and was phoning me direct to make last-
minute plans. He was all ready to travel when Duncan disappeared. This left John with no possible way of buying a
ticket. I suppose I could have foreseen this happening. Duncan was always an unpredictable character, and though we
had got on for the purposes of the whole exciting venture
we had never become great friends. John, the boy who had
answered the newspaper advertisement, had turned out to
be the keenest of my supporters, but in Australia all those
miles away he had no idea what was happening. Without
the backer he had no means of support. He was offered a job
in a sports business and he took it.

Three days later Duncan Parrish turned up again in Sydney, apologizing profusely for his absence on business. It
wasn't easy to take stock of the true situation all those miles
apart, but I had to think things out from the point of view of
the success of the expedition, which had become para-

mount. Duncan had been marvellous throughout all the preparations, sending 600 dollars every two weeks whenever I listed my expenses, and paying for all my telephone calls, but I always suspected he disappeared on purpose at the last moment. He had become somewhat shirty on the telephone about the continual delay to the expedition and the mounting cost. He could be very acid when he wanted. I was feeling pretty acid too. When John cried off, which I had to blame on Duncan's unscheduled disappearance, I had had everything ready for three weeks. I had done it all myself. I was dog-tired but raring to go. Now I was trapped by the weather and I still had the problem of the visa.

What did I feel at this point? I was full of apprehension. I had been on my own in Trengannu in a country which was strange to me with no one to talk to except the Malays, who spoke pidgin English at best. Anyway I had long ago decided not to talk to the Malays about the full extent of my intentions, otherwise the word would have been all over town. Malays love gossip. Now with my visa expired I could be in real trouble if the customs discovered my boat ready for a long trip. At this point there was no question of taking the risk of putting my papers in order. I had come too far along the route and I didn't want any questions asked. But actually I was in a very positive frame of mind. I had lived with the challenge of Kidd's island for so long, I had solved all the problems so far, and I was accustomed to bouncing back whenever the frustration was greatest. I was certainly not going to give up now, not even if Duncan Parrish withdrew his financial support.

But it was more complicated than that. I had set up the expedition at this point and money was not the problem. I was going out into the unknown. I needed his faith in the venture as much as anything, and it was this that niggled me about his absence from Sydney with no forwarding number. There were still practical problems. I was the least experienced sailor of my original crew. I had gained confidence in the last two months in the actual area which I was challenging. I could certainly search and dig for the treasure myself without an accomplice. I didn't expect it to be too deep. But I had no one to hold off intruders in an emergency and no one to remain with the master boat in the Pirate Islands when I took the dinghy on to Hon Tre Lon. If the boat drifted away or was stolen or scuppered I could find myself abandoned within Communist territory with fifty words of the language and no very good explanation anyway. Who would bale me out?

Parrish asked me at this point what I was going to do. It was a real problem. Faced with no alternative I said I would look locally for crew among the backpackers of Trengannu, since I did not want to approach the Malays. I was sure that some of the tourists who had penetrated so far off the beaten track must have an adventurous spirit. I would tap this.

I began to talk to one or two tourists in bars. They were Australians, Germans, New Zealanders, single men with no responsibilities. I told them I was looking for treasure up the gulf, and although they all had the usual response to that, when it came to details they were not so keen. I had to tell them it was in a dangerous area off a Communist country. One fellow who had played along up till that point said absolutely no.

For some time now I think the obvious conclusion had been nagging at my brain. I had discovered the truth about the treasure alone. I had made all the plans alone. I had carried my secret half round the world from California to Mexico, Brazil, Australia and now Malaysia for two years. For most of that time I had been alone. Now I had made the final preparations alone. I alone knew all about my boat and its quirks and had firsthand knowledge of the gulf. There had been nobody to help me when I thought I needed them. I had had plenty of practice in taking the boat out alone and could confidently sail her. I had stowed away the provisions, I had baled out the engine room day after day after storms or merely riding at anchor. I had worn myself out physically through pumping with the handpump two hours or more on a bad day and mentally tangling with Awi and his foreign ways of doing business.

I had two allies at most. One was Captain Kidd, who had revealed to me his secret and whose ghost was still spurring me on. The other was my backer, who had been supportive and generous at least up to his disappearance. I was

champing at the bit to set sail. Everything was carefully
stowed. Everything was ready. There were ample provisions for three people, 150 gallons of fuel and more than
enough fresh water, and the sea conditions had considerably improved. Now I told Parrish that if I could not find a
reliable alternative within the next two days I was going to
attempt to make the trip by myself.

There was an awkward silence at the other end of the
line. Then Parrish spoke. He was cautious and fascinated.
He asked me to give him forty-eight hours to get his business sorted out in Australia, since he was seriously thinking of joining me. It didn't altogether take me by surprise.
In a way it was the obvious solution. Parrish had wanted
to pose as a geologist when we formed the bogus mining
company right at the beginning. I didn't object to him coming along at all. I wanted him to join me – but quickly. We
could sail together in this boat comfortably. He was physically fit, a good swimmer. I decided to give him his forty-
eight hours. All the same something told me he would not
come. Since his disappearance I had become suspicious of
him. I realized I was the only person who had the fullest
confidence in the trip. To the others it was more a question
of material reward. To me that was important, of course,
but the real reward was the trip itself. If I found so much
as a bootlace belonging to Captain Kidd I would have a
bonus. If I found treasure that would be wonderful.

I waited for Duncan's call saying he would join me, but
it didn't come. After two days I called him but he still hadn't
made up his mind. We made another appointment to telephone. Perhaps he would keep it, perhaps not. It was
slowly dawning on me that it did not matter either way.

By now the weather was almost perfect. I sat in the hotel
drinking Carlsberg Special Brew lager, which was my tip-
ple at the time. There was no call by eight p.m., which was
eleven p.m. in Australia. It was getting late for him. He
was unlikely to call now. To hell with him, I thought. I was
itching to go. I wanted to get at least as far as the boat. TFA
1396 was by now my only ally. I took the bus to Chennering, got on board around eleven p.m. and slept. I hadn't
quite made up my mind what to do. I would decide in the
morning.

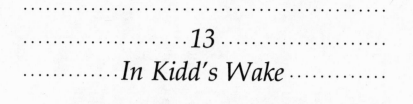

The next morning dawned fine. I weighed anchor and left just as I had done many times on practice trips before. I could simply potter up the coast, overnight on the boat, and return as I had done in the past. Or I could carry on. I set off positively resolving to continue as long as the sea conditions were fair. With my navigation charts spread on the seat in front of the windscreen and my compass already fixed near the wheel I chugged north along the coast of Malaysia towards the Thai border. The sea was moderate but the weather was not brilliant. The craft was relatively stable and I was perfectly at ease handling her; I was happy at last to be on my way, but I figured things were not good enough for me to take the plunge immediately and head straight out to sea. I had several hours of indecision ahead of me. I anchored that night about forty-five miles up the coast and rested. The following day I set off about noon, and by six o'clock that evening, when darkness was about to fall, I had reached Kota Bauru on the Thai border. I didn't feel like turning back. I chugged along for another two hours off the Thai coast and then turned due north into the open sea. The die was cast.

There was a moderate swell and it was a calm and beautiful night. It was an extraordinary position I was in under the sheltering sky of the Gulf of Thailand navigating a small fishing boat possibly right in the wake of Captain Kidd's pirate ship three hundred years before. The kind of vessel Kidd would have sailed would have been about three times larger than mine but that did not mean it was large. It would have been about 100 feet long, a beautiful wooden construction with that sheer wall at the back which was the captain's quarters, similar to Nelson's *Victory*. Unlike my oriental boat, Kidd's certainly had a name. He had made

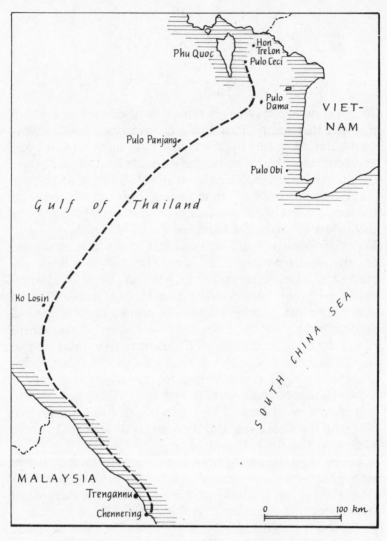

Richard Knight's first trip to Hon Tre Lon

hundreds of voyages in his time but at least three long ones to Madagascar and India as captain possibly of different ships. The name which meant most to me was the *Adventure Galley*. He was commanding that in 1695 when he earned his fatal privateering commission under the Great Seal of England to clear pirates from the Indian Ocean. The *Quedagh Merchant* was one of the ships he brought back to his undoing, laden with riches, but the *Adventure Galley* was always the ship best identified with Kidd. That was the name inscribed on the brass plaque on the lid of the first oak bureau Hubert Palmer discovered in 1931 from which the discovery of all the charts sprang.

Adventure Galley was a good name for a boat on my sort of mission into the unknown. As I sailed, it struck me that I had certain things in common with Kidd apart from the geography of the trip, and I pondered on the similarity of our two destinies. In the darkness and solitude of the oriental night it seemed logical and not at all far-fetched that they should be similar. I knew nothing of Kidd's origins and there were some things I did not really know about my own. I never really knew my own father, who was divorced from my mother when I was very young. He was an accountant and I imagined he would be amused to find me sailing for the treasure trove of a man who had lived on Wall Street.

My stepfather was a gambler. He would certainly have understood and approved of Captain Kidd. He came to live with us when I was twelve and I got on well with him. He was secretary with the Football Combination and later he was secretary of Brighton and Hove Albion. He died ten years later. He had a heart attack as we were sitting in the directors' box at a match. Only my mother, Mrs Blanche Roberts, was alive to see what would become of my quest.

My wanderlust displayed itself early in life, as Kidd's would have done. I lived by the sea and it was impossible not to gaze out and wonder what was there. My first solo trip was on a bus from Shoreham to Worthing when I was eight. I used to go and visit the toy train shop there. Then I went abroad with the Boy Scouts when I was thirteen. That was when Kidd was probably apprenticed and sailed

125

round the world. I went to Switzerland for a holiday. Then I went back to Shoreham Grammar School where I got eight GCE subjects, but I didn't really know what I would do in life. All I knew was that I wanted adventure.

I left school at sixteen and taught myself to ice-skate in Brighton. That was a decisive move but like this one it was quite unheralded. I have said before that I was at school with the son of 'Monsewer' Eddie Gray of the Crazy Gang. Funny that Captain Kidd would bring him back into my life. But I didn't get my show-business connections from Gray. After five months' practising on the ice I auditioned for an ice show in Blackpool, just like that, and was accepted for the chorus. I did two summer shows there and during my National Service I managed to pick up work in the ice show at Wembley Rink, which was near Stanmore where I was billeted. These are the sort of thoughts that come back to you when you are sailing by yourself on the open sea.

When my National Service was finished I saw an advert in *The Stage* for a comedian to work in a summer show in Swanage. I didn't have an act but that's when I did my Danny Kaye impression. They hired me at Swanage for £8 a week as a light comedian and to play parts in sketches. That was in 1955–6.

I was a bit of a freelance, like Kidd. I could do a passable imitation of Danny Kaye's Russian but I was no real linguist. I have a smattering of Portuguese and Spanish – Kidd must have known those. I wondered whether he knew my best language, which was French, thanks to my marriage.

As I sailed I wondered what had become of my wife. I met her in Paris in a bar in 1966; we were married two years later and divorced three years after that. I had gone to Paris to study with Marcel Marceau, the mime artist. A journalist friend of mine knew him and introduced us. I remembered how Marceau told me he was planning to open his own mime school, but at the time the plans were in their infancy. I got a job teaching English in the Berlitz school in Paris. When we were reunited Marceau had already filled his fifteen places, though he allowed me to watch his classes.

I used to go back to England to do pantomime but always in the choruses.

Like Kidd I was also a bit of a stranger in my own land, and my most interesting experiences had always been abroad and were often slightly unorthodox. The highpoint among them till now was probably the one-man 'Evening with Richard Knight' I had organized in Hamilton, New Zealand, about twelve years previously. My acts went well in New Zealand, where I stopped off on a cruise with a girlfriend I had met on the ship and stayed for eighteen months. I made a regular living there in cabaret and children's television. Then one day I wanted something more. I spent my own money on hiring a 2,000-seat theatre in Hamilton for several nights.

The first night was a bit of a disaster, with about 100 people in the house, so the next day I spent the daylight hours touring the housing estates and shopping centres asking everyone if they had seen this international mime artist Richard Knight and his evening of jokes and impressions. No one had, but they all eagerly accepted free tickets. As I handed them the tickets I said shyly: 'As a matter of fact, I am Knight.' They all turned up and the evening was a great success, though I never did get my money back. It was back to small-time cabaret on cruises. That had been my life until now really, a passenger on someone else's boat, but now I was master of my own vessel, my own *Adventure Galley*. More than that, I was captain and crew.

14
The Voyage Out

There was a rock called Ko Losin thirty miles off the coast of Thailand and I made for it. Its flashing light came into view at two in the morning. I knew it had to be Ko Losin, as there was nothing else about. I was terribly excited but also dead tired, and I needed to conserve all my strength if I was to take the big step. I decided to drop a sea anchor in sight of the light and try to sleep for five or six hours so I would be fresh to carry on at first light. You can make a sea anchor out of anything that drags. Mine was made of several jerry-cans three-quarters full of salt water. You hang them off the bow and they act as a brake to stop you drifting with the current. I used no navigation lights and settled a couple of miles off the rock. The only danger was of being run down by a larger vessel, but in my sheltered position I thought this possibility pretty remote for the time being. It was better to chance it than to show a light and wake up finding myself boarded by Thai fishermen. I turned in on the plastic groundsheets I had prepared in the cabin and fell asleep immediately. I didn't expect any interference. I was an innocent vessel in international waters. Only I knew of my plans for the next day.

I woke up with the dawn at 7.30. The weather was not any worse. By now I was quite nervous, excited and anxious to get on. This was the real moment of decision. I had a two-day dash ahead of me. It was now or never. I breakfasted on several cartons of cold coffee. I had a primus stove with me, but it never seemed worthwhile lighting up. It was never very cold, so I had no need for hot food. In fact I was not hungry, though I always get very thirsty at sea. I found myself consuming lots of water and orange squash every time I stopped. I had already established a pattern. I would chug for a couple of hours, then rest for twenty minutes. Around nightfall I would rest for a couple more hours before carrying on under cover of darkness. Then I would put down the sea anchor and sleep in the wide open sea. With no lights I knew I was now taking a risk if I was in the path of any large shipping. It was something I had been aware of ever since Australia. It was commonsense in the seas around Sydney that if you were in a small craft and you saw a tanker you simply got out of its way. Modern tankers are very large and they are mainly navigated by computer on self-pilot. They have an able seaman on look-out but had I encountered a tanker, even supposing the look-out had been able to see anything of me in my tiny boat, his ship would have been too large and slow for him to respond and take avoiding action. Any boat the size of mine would have been sucked beneath its bows. Out there in the open seas I was in no danger from any Communist patrol boats, or from the shallow continental shelf for which I was heading, but I was right in the path of any tanker heading north or south to or from the port of Bangkok. They took a wide berth at least fifty miles off the tip of South Vietnam and continued the arc right into the waters I was now approaching. As usual there was the possibility of an encounter with a fishing boat.

As it was, I saw only a couple of distant vessels for at least twenty-four hours. I used the time to wonder whether I was sailing on a wild goose chase. The idea that any treasure on the island might already have been found had occupied me for three years now. But somehow I didn't think it had. As far as I knew Hubert Palmer, the original finder of Kidd's chart in the 1930s, never went to the Far East and had never been on the island. His brother Guy showed all the maps to close friends but none of them seemed to have worked out the location of Hon Tre Lon. If they had I felt fairly certain there would have been reports of it in the press, especially if anyone had found any treasure.

Soon after the charts were found the world was plunged into the Second World War, when the Japanese overran Vietnam. No one was in a position to get up an expedition then, and I felt fairly confident no one had stumbled on anything under wartime conditions either.

Similarly when the French were fighting the Communists between 1945 and 1954, both sides had other things on their mind than gold doubloons. From 1954 till 1974 the Americans were occupied with Vietnam. It was the same story of unrest all along, and though it didn't preclude someone finding the cache, I was sure that if it had been discovered the news would have filtered to the West. I knew of nothing and I had been into the subject more than anyone else. Certainly nothing had been revealed by the time Rupert Furneaux published *The Money Pit Mystery* in 1972. His conclusions were way off course, but I was fairly certain that nothing had been discovered by anyone else in the ten years between that book's publication and my present trip. What had happened on Hon Tre Lon since the Communists took over in 1974 was a mystery, but one thing is pretty certain, no one since had had access to the literature on Kidd.

Equally mysterious was the island's history before the French took over in 1860. I was fairly confident nothing had been found in the hundred years or so since their occupation, because of the interest in treasure during this time, but what had happened before?

When the French arrived in Vietnam the islands were already known as the Pirate Islands, which suggested that all manner of comings and goings had been recorded under Annamese and Cambodian rule in Kidd's day and since. It was possible that pirates had discovered Kidd's secret or indeed that he had plundered the secret from other pirates and never made the maps himself originally. Kidd might have lived on the island himself and used it as one of his world-wide 'banks'. Or he might have robbed or killed someone who did and confiscated the so-called Kidd charts from him. He might have copied them in his own hand if the British Museum experts were right, for they were sure the charts bore his imprint. He might have gone back for the treasure himself, but somehow I didn't think so. When Kidd offered to show his executioners his plunder in return for his life they had not taken up the offer. I believed the secret had died with him until I identified his island.

On the second day out I saw two or three little ships in

the distance, but they never came close enough to bother me. I was beginning to enjoy myself. The weather was balmy, with just a few specks of rain, and I was entertained by the occasional flying fishes and porpoises and the odd seabird which reminded me I was never very far from the land where I was heading. To the north lay Phu Quoc, a large triangular thirty-mile island to the west of my goal which lies off the Cambodian–Vietnamese border. I had learned in Australia that this island supports some very interesting flora and fauna. One species in particular is unique and found nowhere else in the world – a semi-wild dog with its hair running from back to front.

So I went on. I held a north-north-east course straight towards my next landmark, Pulo Panjang, into the wind, moving slightly to the right every hour or so to counteract the one-knot westerly current I had first heard about back in Singapore. Every couple of hours I emptied fuel from one of my jerry-cans into the fuel tank. I had several tied along the port side to facilitate easy refuelling. I never let the tank get anywhere near empty because I knew from my putterings round Chennering that once this happened and an airlock developed in the engine it could take a long time to start again. There was no danger to life or limb even if I never got it started for the current would take me back to Thailand and since I had stocked up for a crew of four I had food and water to last one man for four weeks. But I didn't want to take any chances, so I kept emptying those jerry-cans. On the first night after Ko Losin I was halfway across the Gulf and travelling smoothly. It was just as Captain Pyett had said it would be.

Pyett was the man who back in Sydney had given us a five-man individually-tailored course including celestial navigation. I thought of him now as the night came in cloudy with the back end of a moon. The question of the phases of the moon had exercised us for a long while during his classes. Ideally of course there would be no moon, he said, but there were cases in which you were better off in an unlit boat sailing with a moon as long as you could keep up-moon of any other vessel. At that point they would be lit from the sky while you would fade into the background,

especially if your boat was a dark colour, blue, for instance,
like mine from Chennering. Pyett had immediately
warmed to his task the moment we told him we were sailing to find treasure. He mapped out three or four routes
over the China Sea and took us over them as if we were
right on the spot. I was following one of them now without
too much difficulty and yet I had been the least diligent of
his pupils. The other guys, who were keen sailors, had
been once a week for six weeks, while I'd skived off a
couple of classes. That is where they had learned all about
SAT-NAV and radar, which was on all the Singapore
yachts, and a shipwreck device which signals to a satellite
and can be picked up even by the Russians. I knew these
things were not necessary. It was not as if I was out on the
open Pacific. I was in a sea scattered with islands where it
was easy to get my bearings. The trouble was half the sea
was in Communist territory, and even now I was nosing
towards Vietnamese waters.

No one really knew where Vietnamese waters started.
The territorial limits of a country are usually set at three or
twelve miles, but Brazil, for example, was currently claim-
ing 200 miles. The problem was knowing what the Vietnamese claimed. If they saw a boat thirty miles off their coast
the chances were they would regard it as a trespasser. This
was an unknown factor, and there were really no pre-
cautions I could take.

At two p.m. I spotted Pulo Panjang on my left. It was a
great relief, for I had been eagerly scanning the horizon for
it for several hours. It was still quite a way away, but it
looked a considerable landmass. It was five miles across
and over 400 feet high. As I had learned from Pyett, one
can judge the approximate distance from a landmass by a
simple equation. It is roughly equal in miles to the square
root of its height in feet. The height was marked on my
navigation chart. My calculations put Pulo Panjang twenty
miles away from me. I took this as an early warning,
because I knew there was radar on its highest point. The
chances are it was not a sophisticated system, but I did not
want to fall foul of the troops garrisoned there. I now had
a definite bearing and turned slightly to the east, heading

north-east for the next island landmark, Pulo Dama, 1,000 feet high, which I should see more or less dead ahead within four hours. I lost Pulo Panjang on my left until it got dark. It took about three hours to get close to Pulo Dama after my first sighting.

By the time I was in its shelter it was quite black and I should have been reassured, but then for the first time I was overcome with real fear. I kept scanning the horizon for the lights of any patrol boats, but there were none. Nor were there any fishing boats, which I would recognize by the little oil-lamps they used as lights in this part of the world. Well after dark I crept along about five miles from the west coast of Pulo Dama, holding a course due north and cutting the engine every twenty minutes or so to listen for the sound of approaching shipping.

Out there in the blackness, with the waves lapping round the hull, one's imagination ran riot. In my mind I thought I heard twenty patrol boats approaching full of Viet guards, but when I cut the engine they faded into the night. The only danger I did not have at that point was the depth of water. There were still twenty fathoms beneath me. I threw out my jerry-cans and sea-anchored for a couple of hours about twelve miles north of Pulo Dama, but I could only get a very fitful sleep.

By three in the morning I had started out again and continued at reduced speed, stopping and starting. I spent an anxious few hours waiting for the light, wondering whether dawn would break over a fleet of patrol boats surrounding me. I knew I couldn't even outrun one of the local fishing boats if it came to a standing start. I prayed there would be nothing, and there was nothing. I was alone in this sea of islands and I determined to anchor within the shelter of one of them, Pulo Ceci, about thirty miles north of Pulo Dama, until night-fall. Still, at first light I was still twelve miles short of that objective and in a very vulnerable position.

Pulo Ceci – latitude 10.13°N, longitude 104.14°E – is a small wooded islet ten miles south-west of Hon Tre Lon, Kidd's island. It is about 400 yards long, rocky and covered with wooded vegetation, and it is connected by a slender reef to a smaller islet a few hundred yards to the south. I had reasoned it was the only spot in the area which afforded reasonably safe cover, as it was isolated several miles away from the other nearest islands.

And then I saw it – Hon Tre Lon amongst its satellites on the northern horizon. It was just like all the other islands, except that I knew it held a secret. After the years of speculation and organization it was a gripping experience to set eyes on it in reality for the very first time. I was very excited. It gave me the boost I needed to continue.

Everything went according to plan. By eight a.m. I had dropped both anchors off the south-west tip of Pulo Ceci in moderately calm and protected waters. There were one or two boats visible at sea but no people on Pulo Ceci itself. I kept scanning the horizon with my 8×50 binoculars for any further signs of activity. Then for the first time in three days I tried to get a few hours of solid uninterrupted sleep. It was hopeless; I was far too nervous. By mid-morning, when I had eaten and rested and drunk a welcome half-mug of brandy, I felt much more confident, even exhilarated. I lazed around below decks and slept hoping that my disguise as a typical oriental fishing boat would protect me till that evening. Though I had no radar on board I did have a short-wave radio which would get the BBC World Service, but I was rarely tempted to turn it on. I was pretty excited. After three years of planning, after all the disappointments, followed by the methodical preparations, after the uncertainties of the sea voyage itself, I could hardly believe that I was only about ten miles from Hon Tre Lon, Grand Pirate Island.

I rested all that day, albeit very fitfully, and started to get together all the equipment I would need for my push on to Hon Tre Lon later in the evening. I had decided to use my little anchorage in the shelter of Pulo Ceci as a home base and complete the last ten or twelve miles in the little twelve-foot dinghy, which would create less of a stir among any islanders who witnessed it than the big fishing boat. There was a north-east wind and some current, so I was anchored about fifty yards off the island to the south-west, which

was quite snug. I ran through the list of my equipment and
ticked each item off as I brought it out of the hold:

1 Microtech 480 metal detector
1 crowbar
1 auger
1 spade
1 set gardening trowels
1 pair binoculars
1½ dozen sacks
2 torches
2 cameras plus film
1 Super Eight cine camera plus film
2 tri-purpose macintoshes, doubling as groundsheets and
    small tent
1 bag assorted tins of food – corned beef, baked beans,
    Kraft processed cheese
1 dozen 250 cc cartons orange juice, coffee etc.
2×1-gal. plastic containers of water
1×5-gal. jerry-can petrol
Extras: anti-mosquito spray, cigarette lighters, batteries,
    knives, spare sun hat, matches, tin opener, cigarettes,
    three bottles Carlsberg Special Brew beer, spare cloth.

By 11.30 p.m. all was ready. Then I pushed the dinghy
over the side, fixed its little four-horsepower outboard
motor and tested it. It started at once, but I was not ready
to leave yet. I loaded the five-gallon jerry-can of petrol, the
metal detector, the auger, the spade, a lifejacket and the
survival kit of food and orange juice and cans of water.
Most of the equipment was brand-new and it was all in
good order.

Then I checked the mother ship, TFA 1396. I refuelled
her main ten-gallon fuel tank, checked the 33-horsepower
engine for oil and as far as possible prepared her for an
immediate getaway on my return. Naturally I showed no
navigation lights.

By midnight everything had been done. I still had two
hours to kill till I thought any islanders would be sound
asleep. I was feeling queasy with nervous tension, though
luckily not seasickness, which rarely affects me. Then on

the dot of two a.m. I set off round the west tip of Pulo Ceci using my pocket compass. The water was calm and protected, and I was feeling confident in my fibreglass dinghy, which was theoretically unsinkable, and in the knowledge that even if the worst came to the worst I would only have a couple of miles to swim ashore.

The one problem was the sound of the dinghy engine. Sound travels a long way at sea, especially in calm conditions. I headed due north-east towards the Pirate Islands. I could see their outline as I puttered on but I kept well away from land so the noise of the engine would not reach any listening ears. I turned and made my approach to Hon Tre Lon from the north, heading for the little North Beach with the triangle on Kidd's chart. The journey from Pulo Ceci had taken about an hour and a half. Then about half a mile out I stopped the engine and started to row towards the shore.

There was no lagoon as on the Kidd map, but this I already knew from French navigation chart 3686. There may have been one in Kidd's time but in three hundred years one can expect a lot of changes in geographical features due to movements on the sea-bed and the tides. It was still cloudy with a little moon, but clear enough to see the beachline just as I had examined it many times with a magnifying glass on the Defense Intelligence Agency aerial photos.

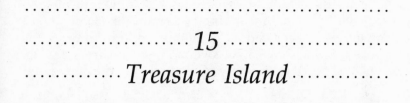

15
Treasure Island

This was the most frightening part of the voyage to date, both very exciting and risky. All I could see was the black outline of the island. I had no idea what was on it apart from, hopefully, the treasure caches. There could have been soldiers on look-out duty for all I knew, but I could see – nothing. There were no boats on the beach, no huts, no lights. Since there were no lights I concluded there were probably no people.

I ran through the other possible dangers. Sharks? Not in this part of the islands. Snakes? I had thought of that but concluded the island was too small. Mosquitoes? Almost certainly. Over the years I have evolved my ways of dealing with them. I use a fan which stops them settling. They do, of course. Then I like to smash them with a wet towel or wait until they are engorged with blood and then crush them on the wrist. The last thing I did before I landed was spray myself from top to toe with mosquito repellent. Then I rowed into the beach, just a strip of sand about seventy yards long at this point as on the DIA photographs.

Behind the beach, back about twenty yards, there was a thick line of vegetation, then the land rose up quickly to the hills. Still I could see no houses or huts. There was no tide or big waves so I left the dinghy lying half in and half out of the water while I stumbled through the sand with a weak torch directed on the ground looking for a place to make a camp. I found a clearing about six yards wide in the vegetation and started to stow my equipment there, wrapped in plastic in case it rained. Then I took off the outboard motor and wrapped that in plastic too. I didn't want that getting wet and delaying my getaway. Lastly I dragged the dinghy up the beach and turned it upside down under the bushes, smoothing its tracks over with a

branch from a tree. It was around 4.30 in the morning by
now and I figured it was about one hour till dawn, so I sat
down with a beer and a cigarette while I ran through the
procedure I had rehearsed over and over again.

Later I noted down the sequence of events in my diary.

Drank one Carlsberg beer. Waited first light. Used binoculars
to check any boats, people, activity in area. None. Taking metal
detector and camera made way tentatively along beach keeping
close to line of undergrowth. 200 yards along turned right – made
way inland. Passed through area of wood and vegetation. 150
yards from beach deposited metal detector in clearing . . .
Climbed part way up small hillside for better view. A few native
dwellings along coast. Took photographs. Returned to clearing . . .

It was an anxious time. I took the metal detector, the
water in a small container, some cheese and luncheon meat
and cigarettes and my binoculars in a canvas shopping bag
from the Trengannu general store and set off in the direction Kidd had indicated. As it became light, I could make
out a thick strip of vegetation stretching about 300 yards in
either direction along the beach. There were still no houses
and no boats and no people.

Then I saw the little island on Kidd's chart in the bay
where the lagoon had been. It was slightly further to the
north than on the chart, but it was there. That was an
exciting moment. I could also see a jetty about fifty yards
long sticking out into the bay. It was obviously in good
repair and had probably been built in the last fifty years
with rock piled up from the beach. I could see too that there
was a dirt track leading back from it which wound up the
hill to the east of the island. There were still no people, but
now I could see some thatched island huts. It put me on
my guard but it was far too late to turn back now.

Now I could see two or three huts. I was walking through
a wood of coconut trees. I knew the map and the legend
by heart and had no need to consult it, but I had copies
in my pocket just in case. I went over the legend I had
deciphered:

360 yards Veer Right North 3 stumps=

55 feet from centre of triangle in Left Rocks
20 feet East of Skeleton of hieb[?]

I had long ago decided that 360 yards was almost certainly taken from the point marked 'anchorage', which placed the cache area about 200 yards from the north shore. After a while I turned into the valley and walked exactly 150 yards. I was carrying a tape measure in my pocket, but I had no need to use it. Ever since Brazil my pacing had been quite accurate. I used to go into the park there and practise pacing 100 yards exactly. So I left the measure in my pocket with the fifty dollars in single bills I had brought along as a possible bribe for any islanders I might meet on my way. I was not looking forward to any such event but I imagined this would soften them up, because the dollar commanded a fantastic black-market rate in Vietnam. At that time it was worth ten times its face value. I was also carrying a few packets of 555 cigarettes, the most popular foreign cigarette in this part of the world.

I was now in the area where, according to the map, I should find three stumps. It was partly wooded, with patches of thick undergrowth, outcrops of rocks and occasional clearings. I looked around for the stumps, but there was nothing. I must have searched for about half an hour. I experienced a bit of disappointment, but I had to admit to myself I had half anticipated this. Now I realized this was how it should be. The stumps were in all probability the trunks of palm trees, which would only have survived about 150 years, and it was very unlikely that the remnants of soft palm wood would survive the elements for three hundred years. They would have disintegrated around 1850, about the time the French first occupied the area.

There was also no sign of a grave or a skeleton, but I comforted myself with the thought that I had never quite fathomed that reference anyway. The most important thing was that I now found myself in an enclosed area of the island which corresponded to the place on Kidd's map where the treasure was marked. In his day he might have needed more precise references, but with my modern equipment, especially the metal detector, I could prospect this place easily during the hours of daylight and locate whatever was there.

It was an area measuring about fifty yards square, sloping up on the west side to a convenient hill which made a look-out post. Before I started work I climbed up to see whether the coast was clear. Again I saw the native huts but I could see no people. I came down again and assembled the three parts of the metal detector. As I had learned on that Australian beach back in Sydney, all ground has some metal content, so the first thing to do was to adjust the sound and visual levels so that only out-of-the-ordinary content would register.

I started walking up and down methodically as if I was mowing a lawn. The ground was covered with grass and wild plants and small bushes, and to my mind it had never been cultivated. There were clear areas and then the occasional small outcrop of rock. I covered all the most obvious places with the detector, especially the clearings, the less overgrown areas and the likely spots around the bases of rocks. I worked for about two hours casting my eyes around constantly for the people I half expected to come upon me. If I saw them first, there was plenty of undergrowth in which to hide, but if they started upon me when I was working I would be completely vulnerable.

One side of the valley I was in was fairly sheltered, but the other, towards the centre of the island, which was also towards where the huts were located, was wide open. The huts were about a quarter of a mile along the north coast beach, separated from my view by a plantation of coconut palms. I started to practise my Vietnamese: *Caio Ko* – 'Hello, girl' – *Ciao-An* – 'Hello, boy.' These were polite forms of address which were likely to make a good impression, according to my boat sisters back in Sydney. 'I am a friend. Please don't tell anyone I am here.' This kept me going till about ten o'clock, but I was feeling pretty despondent because there was no response from the detector.

Suddenly there was an unfamiliar sound. A loud bleep, bleep. I was so apprehensive that it took a moment before I realized what it was. The metal detector! It was reacting

140

strongly. I became madly excited. I was sure I had struck gold. In the three years that I had thought about the treasure day and night in the face of endless scepticism from others I had always convinced myself that it was still there. I was proud enough of myself for having identified the island correctly and interpreted the chart; the idea that I was about to get a bonus in the form of fortune was almost more than I could bear. Yet the evidence was there. The metal detector refused to go silent. It was registering over a large area about four yards by three.

I laid it down under some bushes and raced up the hill to my look-out post before I did anything else. There was no one to be seen. Now I ran back to the beach to get my tools, spade, garden trowels and auger. It was after ten in the morning by now and the tropical sun was high in the sky, but I scarcely noticed the hard work as I covered the 400 yards to my depot at the beach and back in twenty minutes with my heavy equipment. Before I started to dig I went up the hill once more, this time with my binoculars. I was expecting to see fishing boats in the distance, which would in a way have been a reassuring sight, since it would mean that the men were off the island, even though I knew they could come back once they had made their catch and that their womenfolk were still ashore. I saw nothing.

I started to think about my own boat back in the shelter of Pulo Ceci. Would other fishermen find it, or worse still the Communist patrol? It would be too ironic if I returned with the treasure to find the big boat that would carry me to Malaysia gone. I would be cast adrift in a dinghy on an unfriendly sea.

Before I thought like that I had to find the treasure, and before I found the treasure there was hard work to be done. Then a shadow of doubt crossed my mind. The French had used Hon Tre Lon as a military base during their eighty-year occupation of Vietnam. They were bound to have left evidence of this around. Supposing I had simply located a deposit of cases of ammunition? Even worse, supposing I had stumbled across a mine? Too bad, was my reaction to that. After all the effort, the preparation, the disappointments, the considerable risks, I was here in Kidd's island. It was do or die.

I chose a place right in the middle of the site and assembled my auger till it was operational as a corkscrew drill. The first rod measured two foot six, and I tried it first, but it was obviously too short. There was nothing significant in its path. I put on an extension which sank it down to five feet, but still I did not strike lucky. I tried down to seven feet. Nothing. This was very disappointing. If the treasure lay much deeper in the ground, at ten or twelve feet perhaps, it would take me hours to dig for it on my own.

I pulled the drill up and started again about eighteen inches to the left. It took me about ten minutes to wind the shaft down again and get it to about four feet. I pulled it out – and this time there was something. There were little chips of wood in the blade of the auger, and they were obviously man-cut.

It is difficult to describe my state of mind as I made this discovery. Had I really found Captain Kidd's 313-year-old treasure? I was pretty excited. It was similar to finding one-self with eight draws on the treble chance and wondering what the first dividend is going to be. I was like a cat on hot bricks, eager to be on with the task and eager also to be a million miles away. The more evidence of the treasure I found, the more apprehensive I felt about detection.

I took the Malaysian machete I had brought from Tren-gannu and started to hack away at the undergrowth all round the area. Then I took my pointed garden spade and started to dig. It was hot and dusty work, but it was not all that difficult. The ground was dry and sandy and I made quick progress. I had been digging for about three quarters of an hour when my spade struck something hard. I peered down into the hole, which by now was about four feet deep in the centre. I had hit something dark and solid. I felt with my fingers and realized it was wood. I brushed off the earth all round the area and what I revealed was a fantastic piece of authentic history.

It was a dark, old oak chest which would have been old even in Kidd's time. For Kidd it was to whom it had

142

belonged, I felt sure. It was Kidd's own chest. The lid was almost black, gnarled and cracked. I built out the sides of the pit to get a better look at it. It measured approximately three foot six inches by two, though it looked much bigger lying down there in the semi-darkness. I was hoping for an inscription which would make my chest the twin of Hubert Palmer's, or would at least offer some form of identification. There was no inscription, no writing, no initials, no identification at all, only some metal bands to reinforce it, and in the centre of the lid a single lock by which it was closed tight.

I stared at my find for a long time. Even now I could be cheated out of the treasure. The chest could be empty. I didn't wait to pick the lock but took a crowbar to it, and what followed was probably the most glorious moment of my life. Complete justification. I had found Kidd's pirate treasure.

What was in the chest? For a while I didn't touch. I just stood and looked. It was pieces of eight, just as you would expect – coins of every description and size, in gold and silver and copper. There were European ones, mainly Dutch and Portuguese of varying dates between 1650 and 1660. And there were oriental coins, Annamese, Chinese and Korean, circular with their distinctive square holes in the middle for stringing on tally sticks. The chest was three-quarters full, which meant I was looking at a fortune.

I dug my fingers down into the coins and let them filter through, but there was no time to waste. Whilst unearthing this chest I had struck a second chest with my spade, just about six inches to the left, and I hastened to uncover this one too. It was plain now that the first auger drilling which had revealed nothing had gone between the two chests.

The second chest was the same size, shape and colour as the first. Again it had no inscription, but this time it had two locks instead of one. I gave the lid the same crowbar treatment and this time I was rewarded with an even more marvellous sight. What was in the chest can only be described as spectacular. This time it was about two-thirds full of works of art, of vases, figurines, little buddhas, statuettes made out of the most exquisite oriental jade and porcelain, many of them of the Ming dynasty.

I spent half an hour just lifting them gently out of the place they had rested for three centuries. I examined them, admired them, just touched them. One in particular caught my imagination, a beautiful six-inch figurine in pink jade of a bearded Chinese sage standing next to a tree, one arm joined to the trunk as if it was a branch. Then there was a matched pair of square green jade bases mounted with tiger dogs, their heads twisted round over their shoulders.

I dug deeper to reveal a mass of Dutch and Portuguese gold and silver coins, at least 500 of them mixed in with oriental ones as before. That was not all. Beneath the coins lay three dozen gold bars, each measuring about $5'' \times 1\frac{1}{2}'' \times \frac{1}{2}''$, and beneath the gold were several lengths of printed oriental fabric pressed so flat over the years that it seemed like a solid mass at first.

The find in this chest was absolutely priceless. I was lost in reverie and almost forgot where I was and the danger I might be in. It was time to go up once more to my look-out post and scan the horizon with my binoculars.

What I saw did not reassure me, for this time I was not alone. There were a couple of fishing boats about three quarters of a mile out to sea, and what was worse I could also see one or two occupants of the huts along the coast. I had to hurry and get the treasure under cover, but I realized there was no way I could use the daylight hours to make my getaway. I obviously had to wait for nightfall.

I went back to the pit and was about to start taking the pieces out of the chest when something made me change my mind. I had found the second chest by chance. Now what if there was a third? Just in case, I decided to open up the pit to the left and right of the chests I had discovered. Again my gamble was justified.

This time I came across a smaller chest, measuring about eighteen inches by fifteen, but this contained the most valuable find of all. The small chest was full of jewellery, amulets, gold and silver rings, several with set stones. Within the chest there was another, smaller box. This contained cut diamonds, emeralds, a ruby weighing around sixty carats and other gem stones. Kidd's plunder took my breath away.

Many people to whom I have related this story personally since have asked the obvious questions. How did you feel? What were you thinking? I was truly extremely thrilled. But above all, regardless of the contents of the chests, I felt the immense satisfaction of having proved that Kidd's treasure trove existed. It was a justification of all the research and the strife over the past few years. I thought back to the three attempts I had made to get permission to enter Vietnam legally, to the fictitious geological and mining company, the archaeological expedition and the proposed tourist visit.

More than that, it was a justification of my original brainwave in discovering the identity of the island itself. Had the chests contained only Captain Kidd's hat and boots it would have been sufficient reward. It was a wonderful experience.

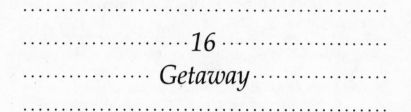

16
Getaway

For a while I just relaxed in the knowledge I had Kidd's treasure. I snacked on Greatwell luncheon meat, processed cheese and three cartons of orange juice.

It was a beautiful view from this spot. Beyond the beach a chain of small islands stretching away to the Cambodian mainland about twelve miles to the north was silhouetted against the calm blue sea. It was extraordinarily tranquil, like a peaceful morning on the Sussex Downs, a fine day with blue skies, some cloud and a mild breeze. I must have spent a good hour suspended in a state of wonderful exhilaration, but I was becoming aware again of my precarious position. It was time to get back to work. I took the metal detector and worked round the edge of the chests, but now it was silent. From my research and study of Kidd's charts I was sure I had not found all the buried treasure; I thought there were as many as three more caches in the valley. I determined to search for these later, time and circumstances permitting. For now I reminded myself that if I was not careful I stood to lose everything I had. I was faced with the practical problem of getting what was a cumbersome as well as dazzling haul under cover before anyone stumbled on me and my secret. I photographed the contents of each chest in detail as quickly as possible and decided to be on my way.

It was now one o'clock, and the islanders I had seen would probably be taking a siesta after their mid-day meal. It was as good a time as any to be on my way so I could have everything ready in order to leave the island under cover of darkness.

Reluctantly I started to pack things up, putting first the heavy coins in the sacks I had brought with me for the purpose and then the delicate porcelain vases. The sacks weighed me down and I had to make at least six trips back-wards and forwards to the dinghy, carrying two sacks each trip and with each about one-third full, before I had every-thing in the shade of the bushes at my hiding place near the beach.

I sat down and rested. This was the most difficult time of all. Although I was pretty exhausted, my mind refused to rest. One minute I wanted to cry out: 'Success! I've found it!' The next I reminded myself how important it was to remain undetected, or everything would go to waste. It was early afternoon and I desperately felt like a drink, indeed several. I kept telling myself it would be stupid in the circumstances to get happily drunk, as I would fall asleep for hours in my present state of fatigue.

One thing which kept nagging at me was whether or not to bother to cover the hole. It meant breaking out of my cover again during the hours of daylight. On the other hand, that hole was living testimony that someone had been there, and I presumed the islanders knew enough about their small island to know it was not one of them. The chests, which I had had to leave in the bottom of the pit because they were too heavy to remove and take with me, were proof that something had been found in the hole. Would the islanders, possibly aware, like the Oak Island locals of Nova Scotia, of ancient pirate legends, put two and two together and look for other caches in the valley? Or would they simply raise the alarm and try to find me? I did not know whether they had any inter-island communi-cations, but I did know that I was vulnerable for a couple of days yet. That was how long it was going to take me to get well outside Vietnamese waters – always supposing my mother boat was still anchored off Pulo Ceci.

I lay there agonizing over the question of discovery until halfway through the afternoon. I had another bite to eat, a cigarette, re-sprayed my skin with mosquito repellent, and lay there trying to rest and fondly examining some of the artefacts again. Then I made the decision to fill in the hole. I went carefully back to the valley and re-filled it with the loose earth I had taken from it. Although the site was still detectable I figured that all but the most curious would pass it by. By the time I had finished with it it looked like a large animal grave.

I looked at my watch. It was five p.m. I was now ready to get back to the mother ship, but I couldn't leave the island shore without cover of darkness, which meant I had about an hour and a half to kill here in enemy territory. I would do myself no good sitting in my hideaway worrying again, and there was an alternative. I could look for the other caches. According to my calculations and Kidd's maps, the second cache should be 150 yards away from the first. I paced it out and took the metal detector.

This time I did not have to experiment for a couple of hours. I fairly soon got a reading over a larger area than before – about six yards by four. I put the auger down in the centre and again I struck lucky. When it came up this time there were the same wood chips in the blade, plus something new – little bits of porcelain.

I was in an agony of temptation. Judging by my previous experience I would have about two hours' digging in front of me. By that time it would be dark and I would have to sleep on the island and continue the next day. I did not dare dig by torchlight now I knew Hon Tre Lon was inhabited. I was exhausted from my digging already; but it was another matter that decided me. I just wanted to get away with what I had found to date. Quite apart from the risk of detection and of the impounding of my boat, which seemed to be increasing hour by hour, there was a limit to how many of the precious things I could load into my little dinghy. After all I had been through, it would be plainly tragic to lose the lot at the bottom of the South China Seas.

The euphoria of the second find wore off quickly with this reasoning, and I made my way back to the beach to wait out the rest of the hour and a half till dark. As soon as it was quite dark I dragged the dinghy down to the water's edge and loaded it with the sacks, balancing them very carefully. I rowed out into the bay and away from the island. I rowed much further than I had done on the incoming journey, and as soon as I had put enough distance between me and Hon Tre Lon to muffle any sound I threw away the auger, spades and the gardening equipment, to lighten the load. I had others on board the master ship. The one thing I did not throw away was the metal detector.

I got the outboard motor started easily in the calm water and slowly and fearfully made my way back to Pulo Ceci. My mission was nearly completed but I wasn't at all sure what I would find when I got to the other island – if I would find anything. Would my boat still be there? Would a patrol boat be tied up beside it? Would it be swarming with Vietnamese officials or fishermen?

I still went slowly to reduce the engine noise. I was also pretty weighted down and did not want to risk taking on water and capsizing. The trip in had taken over two hours, but I took double that getting back to Pulo Ceci. I rounded the tip about midnight. Then I saw the dark outline of the mother ship against the night sky. It was a beautiful sight. I watched the gap close between the two boats with mounting excitement. The treasure was mine. All I had to do was to get it into the three roomy holds of the Malay fishing boat.

I loaded the precious sacks on board and stowed them carefully in the front hold, covering them with fishing gear, empty sacks, rope and old nets. I put the metal detector away and hoisted the dinghy on to the deck. I opened two or three cans of beer and even started on a bottle of brandy, but again I knew I was being foolhardy. I crashed for a couple of hours and when I awoke paid for my leisure with a few minutes' panic when I could not raise one of the anchors. After that I started off hell for leather for Pulo Dama.

This time I threw caution to the winds. I didn't steer a careful course, I steered a straight one – right out of these unfriendly waters towards the open sea. I saw the silhouette of the Pulo Dama islands and passed five miles to its west just as it was getting light. Still I didn't stop. I had to pass through a four-mile area strung out with islands and I knew I would be visible up to fifteen miles from Pulo Dama itself. But I knew too that the villages were at shore level and that their visibility was no more than five miles. It was just a question of risking it and running their gauntlet.

I kept going until night-time with occasional stops. Then

one hour after dark I put out the sea anchor and had my first real celebratory drink. I was sixty miles off the coast of Vietnam. I was relaxed, glowing; I even shed a few tears of happiness. I drank most of the bottle and then slept for six hours until daybreak. Then I was off again, this time with the north-east wind and the waves behind me. It was time to reflect on just what I had in the hold, I went over it again and again and I began to list it.

First chest:
– Coins. The majority Chinese and oriental in base metal, brass, copper etc. Some European coins, mainly gold and silver.

Second chest:
– About one dozen statuettes, buddhas and figurines. Oriental. Jade – green, black and pink. Average height 4–10″. The most interesting being the chinaman and the tree and the two tiger dogs.
– Approximately two dozen vessels. Eastern. Mainly porcelain. Various sizes and shapes 4–12″. Half white and blue Ming. The rest multi-coloured.
– Several folded fabrics – eastern design, about 6′×3′.
– Approximately thirty gold bars – 5″×1½″×½″.
– About 200 gold coins and a lesser number of silver. European and eastern.

Third chest:
– Several silver, gold and alloy bracelets, armlets, necklets, some with set stones.
– Small wooden box containing jewels, approximately two dozen, badly cut by today's standards but invaluable.
– 1×60-carat ruby (possibly spinal or zircon)
– 4×5–15 carat diamonds (quartz?)
– 4×6-carat emeralds
– Various other stones, several cabuchon-cut.
– Approximately two dozen small gold pellets – or balls – with minute inscriptions including elephant heads.
– Approximately 20 rings, some with set stones, cabuchon-style.

I later estimated the value of the entire contents as being around £40m based on the jewellery content of the third chest.

I did not know that within thirty-six hours I would undergo a far more dangerous experience than I had so far, and that I would be within an ace of losing everything I had.

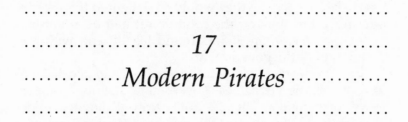
Now I actually had the treasure, I began to see my problems were not over. A passage from Ian Fleming's *Man with the Golden Gun* kept coming into my mind. It is one of my favourite books and I had read it so many times that whole chunks of it were committed to my memory. One of them seemed particularly appropriate to my situation now. Like me, James Bond has unravelled a mystery and is sitting on a goldmine, but will he live to tell the tale?

James Bond wiped his ear and the bottom of the glass with his handkerchief. It was almost unbearable. He had heard his own death sentence pronounced, the involvement of the K.G.B. with Scaramanga and the Caribbean spelled out, and such minor dividends as sabotage of the bauxite industry, massive drug smuggling into the States and gambling politics thrown in. It was a majestic haul in area Intelligence. He had the ball! Could he live to touch down with it? God, for a drink!

James Bond's fate was in the hands of Ian Fleming and one could be reasonably sure that he was indestructible. I did not have the same assurance in real life. Even if I made it out of enemy territory, I was still not out of the rough. How would I get the treasure into the West, and what was I going to do with it?

The problem of its disposal had already entertained our minds for a long time in Australia. I have said before that I would like to see it displayed together as one find in a museum for everyone to see. I knew of no pirate stash which had been kept together in this way. I thought it would be of immense historical value. But there was at least one museum I favoured which saw my treasure as ill-gotten gains. The Smithsonian in Washington, which I had already approached before leaving for Vietnam, had written back to me saying they would be delighted to make an offer for it but only on the condition it had been got out of the country where it was found legally and with the permission of the government.

This was clearly not possible to obtain – I had decided not to approach the Vietnamese government. It would come as news to them that I had it now. Now it dawned upon me exactly what would be the reactions of other countries when I tried to take a valuable collection of coins, gold bars and hand-worked artefacts into their territory. In Chennering, for instance, the port I had sailed from just about a week ago, they were likely to regard me with great suspicion given that my visa was now well overdue. There was no guarantee that they would not search my boat. Though there was always talk of treasure in the South China Seas, that would not be their first thought. That would be drugs. Many a tourist boat is given a good going over in that part of the world. A westerner sailing a fishing boat within easy run of the opium triangle would give them lots to think about. They would not find drugs, but they would find a sixty-carat ruby. Within the small box which had been concealed within the smallest chest there were perhaps two dozen loose precious stones, including diamonds and emeralds, and, most valuable of all, this huge rich red stone which probably originated in Burma, where all the grade-one rubies come from. Such a find would blossom into a huge international incident which I simply could not risk.

It was obvious that the treasure in its entirety could not enter Malaysia through Chennering. I started to plan which pieces I would conceal about my person and risk a run through the customs into Singapore. I particularly liked the little Chinese man. He would have to go with me. Surely I could find room for some of the gold bars and of course a handful of gold coins. I chugged across the gulf dreaming along these lines and entering my thoughts in my diary. It was not my most favourite occupation, writing it up, and it was always two or three days behind. Still, now I had something really exciting to confide I scarcely noticed where the time went.

I was sleeping a good six hours at night and cutting a fine dash across the gulf by day, making much faster time than on the outward trip. When I felt like a bath I tipped a bucket of seawater over my head. My pleasure would have been complete if I had been able to take a dip in the sea, but I knew that it is the most dangerous thing a lone sailor can do. A current may take him away in seconds or a wind carry the boat away. Even with a crew, the engine should always be kept running, just in case. I made do with my improvised shower. I smoked, I drank and wrote and rested and gazed out of the wheelhouse at my unseen destination.

On the second morning I noticed a speck on the horizon. It developed into a black box and became a Thai fishing boat. All through the voyage I had feared the intrusion of the notorious Thai pirates; now I had to decide what I would do if this boat turned out to be them. I decided not to make any abrupt movements but to meander off at a tangent from them as if I had always been thinking of changing my course. On my new course we should have passed two miles apart, but the Thai vessel turned in my direction. After ten minutes it was obvious that it was closing in on me. I carried on. After twenty minutes it became clear they planned to intercept.

My first thought was for my gun. After all the discussion about what to do in case of emergency, I had finally taken one rather half-hearted precaution in Trengannu. I had bought myself a black plastic toy gun at the local toyshop. I left it behind when I took the rowing boat to the island, because I realized it wasn't going to do any good at all. Now I felt around for it. Then I remembered the story of the French wife who had been shot dead as soon as she produced a weapon. I hastily abandoned that idea and put my gun away.

I decided to act the innocent, even the welcoming tourist. This would call on all my acting experience. I wasn't feeling at all welcoming. When they were about half a mile away I stopped my motor and I got down on my knees and said a prayer. Perhaps it was answered. Suddenly I knew that what I had to do was to make myself as conspicuous as possible to give them a sense of security. I climbed on deck in front of the wheelhouse and stood with my arms down by my sides so they could clearly see I had no weapons. In front of me was the hold containing the sacks full of Kidd's jewels. Next to them were the sacks with the coins. During our navigation courses we had discussed many times what to do on just such an occasion as this. I knew it was important not to panic. But it was just as important not to be ridiculously friendly. We had distilled the correct attitude down to 'Smile and hold your ground'.

I watched the Thai boat come closer and counted six men on board. I could see three through the windows of the cabin. The other three were on deck. It was a big boat, about seventy foot, twice as large as mine, and it towered above mine as it drew alongside. The three Thais on deck jumped down on to my deck. My throat was dry, but I managed a few words. 'Do you speak English?' I asked, rather warmly in the circumstances. There was no reply, so I repeated the question. Again no response. This time I took out my cigarettes.

By now the three Thai sailors were lined up before me. I opened the pack and offered one to each of them. Only one took one; still it was enough to break the ice a little. I was shaking like hell and wondered what on earth would happen when we tried to light them. Then the man in the middle pointed to my wrist-watch. It was a nice watch, though not expensive, a cheap oriental self-winding job; still I was not sorry to lose it and gladly took it off – not too eagerly, but purposefully. I handed it to the man who coveted it. I thought he became a little more human, though it was completely impossible for me to read any more subtle expressions in their faces. They were blank cruel masks, and I was by no means confident they wouldn't try violence on me next.

The man with the watch was occupied with playing with it while the other two went into the wheelhouse, presumably to find some little memento for themselves. They found several. First the bottles of whisky which I had thoughtfully laid in store for just an emergency like this; then some cartons of cigarettes; then my three cameras and radio; and then their eyes lighted on my green metal cash box. To the mind of a Thai sailor a cash box meant cash. They were briefly annoyed because they could not open the box, but they took it away anyway. For me it was a particularly sad moment, because I knew the box contained something much more interesting than money. It contained all the exposed film I had shot on the island. When I uncovered the treasure, I had shot four rolls of colour film and two cine films before the sun went down. I had photographed everything, the chests and the island and the treasure as it looked when I first found it, and several of the items individually and some set pieces with my favourite figurines in groups.

When the Thais found that box I was on the point of protesting, but I quickly realized it might have been dangerous, for they clearly intended to take anything they wanted, whatever I had to say. Reluctantly I said goodbye to the film. I have often wondered what they did with it; indeed I made a few inquiries among the fishing fraternity when I later got to Thailand. There is a big black market in film and camera equipment, but most of this was exposed and no use to resell in the ordinary market. When they found out what it was, they probably threw it overboard into the sea – my pictures of something no one else has ever seen since the days of Captain Kidd.

Still those little finds saved my life and saved the treasure itself which was still below decks. They handed everything back to their colleagues on board the fishing boat and left me alone. The whole incident took about seven minutes. They might easily have killed me out of frustration with their small haul, they might easily have searched the boat and found the treasure, though I had taken the precaution of covering it with sacks and fishing tackle, so that a quick glance revealed nothing. If they had, they might still have killed me.

As it was I think they were confused to find a westerner on a humble fishing vessel, and this is what saved me. I was obviously not carrying Vietnamese refugees with all their possessions, and I wasn't a rich American yacht. For ten minutes I watched them getting smaller and smaller out of the corner of my eye and couldn't believe my luck. The whole incident prepared me for the next time I was intercepted, six hours later, by another similar boat. It was mid-afternoon this time and two sailors came on board. This time I didn't wait for them to search. I had 200 dollars ready in my hand which I handed over immediately. We were almost effusive with each other – 200 dollars is a lot of money to a Thai fisherman. They left immediately. The next time I parted with anything would be when I was good and ready.

By five p.m. that evening I was nearly ready. I had my approximate bearing in the gulf, and I knew I could not sail right into the possible hands of the customs officers in Chennering or any other port. By now I had decided that if I could not take all the treasure in, I should take nothing at all.

During my many discussions with Duncan we had debated about breaking it up and offering it piecemeal if we could not get a deal with a museum. The Smithsonian might not want it, but I had not ruled out the Getty Museum in Malibu, California. I had heard that the Getty Museum already had on display some pieces which were come by illegally and were the subject of a claim from the Turkish government, and I presumed they might make an offer for Kidd's hoard based on a proper valuation by experts such as Sothebys. To get that valuation, I thought it was important to keep the treasure together. After all we could always break it up afterwards. What I had retrieved was a historical gem. People's greed always seemed to be their undoing and in the end they were left with nothing. I had heard that some of Blackbeard's treasure had been unearthed in the 1930s, but where is it now? Broken up and gone. I had no idea at the time just how I was going to get it to Sothebys; but I knew I was going to have a damn good try.

All in all, there seemed only one course open to me for the time being, and that was to do as Kidd did – bury the treasure and come back for it when I was better organized. I toyed with lots of ways of disposing of it. With water all around I thought perhaps I would place it under the sea.

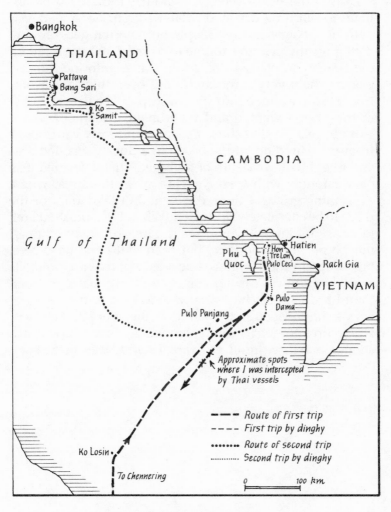

*Richard Knight's first and second
trips to Hon Tre Lon*

That seemed to entail many risks, and the greatest was that it might be destroyed by this new element or would be very difficult to relocate and recover.

During the next twenty-four hours, I knew I was destined to put it on dry land. I later sought out a wild area with no villages and no people but enough geographical distinguishing features for me to memorize. I anchored off the beach and started unloading things into the dinghy, placing them very carefully, doing everything in reverse from Hon Tre Lon. It took me two trips till I had everything in the place I wanted and then about three hours' hard work burying it all. I chose a place about forty yards away from the waterline off the beach in a thickly wooded area and dug down to a depth of four feet. Then I covered it all over carefully with loose vegetation. In that area, where everything grows, I figured it wouldn't take long for the place to be completely disguised. When I had finished I felt rather sad. I knew I would see the treasure again, though maybe not for some time; but then that must have been how Captain Kidd felt too. I decided not to write down its exact location, in case anyone found my maps as I had found Kidd's. His chart was what led me to the treasure. It was simple enough to memorize the spot I had chosen. I wouldn't forget it, for I planned to come back much sooner than three hundred years. I started back to the boat.

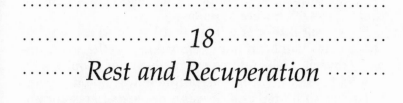

Some days later I arrived in Chennering. The owner of my boat was delighted to see it back. It was worth about 10,000 dollars, and that is quite something to a Malaysian fisherman. But I didn't stop around to celebrate with him. No questions were asked, and I started regretting my decision not to try and import a few chosen pieces, the pink buddha statuette and some vessels and gems. Still I knew I had to go through several customs checks shortly.

I put the regrets behind me and decided to go to the Malay capital, Kuala Lumpur, for a little rest and recreation of my own. I checked into a little hotel in the Chinese quarter and started to let off steam, but first I telephoned Duncan in Australia. His first reaction was one of relief to hear from me. He thought something had gone badly wrong. It was only as an afterthought that he asked me what had become of my plans to get the treasure. 'I've got it,' I said. There was a stunned silence from Sydney. 'You're joking,' he came back.

He made me tell him all about it bit by bit and I did so over the course of the next three days. He was terribly excited and very practical and promised to work on the plans for disposing of it. We had to consider all eventualities: what if the Vietnamese claimed it; what if they won the treasure in the international courts; and what, which was the most likely thing of all, if everyone in the world called Kidd staked a claim to their ancestor's ill-gotten gains. We decided they would have no chance. Apart from proving direct descent, they would have to supply documented evidence that the treasure positively belonged to Kidd, and that he had legally acquired it. Then Duncan asked me if I needed money and agreed to send me some. We were so close to our goal, and neither of us suspected any of the difficulties which were to follow.

For myself it was only now that I realized some of the strain that I had been under embarking on the adventure all by myself. I telegraphed my mother after about a week and told her of my triumph, but there was no one I could talk to about it firsthand. It was a new experience for me, a natural loner, but for the first time I knew what it was like to crave company. I was totally exhausted, physically and emotionally, and got very drunk for some days. I plucked up courage and decided to face the music over my expired visa – now six weeks overdue – to leave Malaysia and go to Singapore.

What followed fully justified my decision to leave items of the treasure behind. I no longer thought wistfully of the pink buddha as my bags were searched, and my clothes, and more, on the border town of Jahore Baru across the causeway from Singapore. If any valuable artefacts or coins had been found by the customs I should have had to provide a receipt or at the very least a plausible explanation of where I had got them, and that might easily have led to embarrassing questions and further investigations. As it was, they found nothing, but they didn't give me an altogether easy time. It was five p.m. when I was stopped and searched by the customs officers, and twenty-four hours later when I was allowed on my way. I spent the night in the town, but my luggage spent the night in the customs shed and I had to go and see the Chief of Police about my overstay before I was finally let out of the country.

In Singapore I checked into another tiny hotel but my need for company grew. It was more than a need to get my pent-up emotions and the saga of my adventures off my chest; I needed an educated assessment of what I had achieved and what was the best way forward. Duncan Parrish had left all the press coverage and story rights to me, wanting only his share of the treasure and his anonymity. I decided to contact David Watts, the *Sunday Times* correspondent in Singapore. Of course he was extremely interested to learn of what was essentially a very good story. He got me drunk, and I got him drunk, which was more difficult. All in all we spent a lot of time together and I told him everything in detail. It was my own fault, but I was to regret the pressure that it brought down upon me in the subsequent months. Suddenly everyone wanted to advise me on my affairs and I, who had wanted time to relax and think, found myself flying half round the world back to London to sign a contract with the newspaper. In the event the contract was never signed, but I am grateful to the Features Editor, Colin Simpson, for making it possible for me to take it easy for a while in England again and for at least one amusing incident along the way.

Colin, who met me at the airport, lived at Oxted in the Surrey countryside and booked me into a nearby motel to recover from the flight. It was about midday when we arrived. 'Have a little rest,' he said, 'and come down in about half an hour. There is someone I should like you to meet over lunch.' When I came down I found Colin at the bar with a distinguished-looking, cultured gentleman of about seventy wearing a full beard. 'Ah, Richard,' Colin said to me amiably, 'this will interest you. Our friend here is an authority on Captain Kidd and the seventeenth-century pirates.' Later I was to take issue with this, since he claimed to have the only contemporary portrait of Kidd hanging in his home. I was sure it was not authentic, because there simply was no record of any contemporary portraits of Kidd. I couldn't take issue with what Colin said next, however. 'Richard Knight, I want you to meet Richard Knight.'

Gradually it became clear to me that I wanted to tell my own story and not be beholden to a newspaper. Suddenly everybody seemed to have a part of me and I was no nearer getting where I wanted to be, which was back in South East Asia to expose my find to the world. I consulted with some old friends, a group of Manchester-based businessmen I had known since the days of the Blackpool ice shows. They wanted to form me into a business and had a programme of lecture tours mapped out for me to give right round the world.

I was not at all sure that this was my role, but our discussions that summer gave me the opportunity to relax in the little country cottage they offered me near Bury, and it turned out to be a most happy period. I continued to read about Captain Kidd wherever I could, notably on my trips to London in the British Library and at the Houses of Parliament, where I went to look at the original documents about his case, which was handled before it came to trial by the Lord Bellomont whose family features are familiar to us from an eighteenth-century portrait by Joshua Reynolds. In his papers of 1700, the year before Kidd's execution, I found the reference to his speaking with a Scottish tongue.

I recovered from the attentions of the press, and, though I did not know it at the time, they would have their story when I was arrested. David Watts went into print in the *Daily Telegraph* on 5 September 1983, about six weeks after the Foreign Office informed my mother that I was detained in Vietnam. Colin Simpson was even quicker off the mark. He telephoned my mother in July, following the story in the *Mail*, and his articles appeared in the *Sunday Times* two weeks running the following month. Their interest was followed by a lot of programmes on local radio stations, including Radio Sussex, Radio Brighton and Southern Sound. And by a friend of Colin Simpson's in Los Angeles, Robert Bloggs, who worked for *People* Magazine.

Bloggs became most inquisitive and my mother did not want to answer his intimate questions without the magazine making some contribution towards my release. This they declined to do, but Bloggs himself did keep in touch with my mother and helped keep her spirits up with rumours of American television interest. My mother meanwhile was writing to everyone in sight, from the *News of the World* to Robert Maxwell. There were no spectacular contributions to the fund, however, and it limped along in fivers, not hundreds or thousands, its progress largely due to the efforts of my schoolfriend Gray. Though I didn't know it while I was idling the summer away in Manchester, I was about to embark on another very dangerous trip.

I had frequently telephoned Duncan in Australia during the summer months about the recovery and disposal of the treasure. Suddenly he phoned to say he had solved it all. It was September. Duncan and I had always been like-minded about the expedition and its rewards, and it was in a high state of excitement that I flew back to the Far East that October at his expense to renew our business deal. I was to get things rolling in Bangkok while he obtained a yacht and put together a crew in Australia. One thing was certain this time – we intended to go back for our treasure in a certain amount of style. We talked about going back to Hon Tre Lon too to recover the second cache of which I had found evidence in the blade of the auger, but in the end we decided to concentrate on what we already knew about in detail – the ten sacks of Kidd's treasure I had reburied somewhere on the west coast of the Gulf of Thailand.

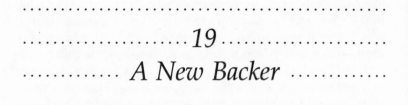
The preparations took longer than we expected. It was not until the New Year that the yacht set sail for Singapore with a crew of two Australians and an Englishman. I would join them in the Far East.

The deal with this crew was the same as with the first, although they had none of the same risks or the worry. It should have been an easy voyage with a pot of gold at the end of it. They were just off Singapore when the first disaster struck. The brother of one of the Australians was badly injured back home in a motorbike accident, and he wanted to fly home and be with him. Our expedition was postponed while I searched Singapore for a replacement, but then a second disaster struck, with much more far-reaching consequences. My backer Duncan, who had been with me for nearly two years, simply disappeared.

Duncan had been uncontactable before, of course, and I was used to his unpredictable ways. He was, like me, a loner, and I had grown to accept this and to respect him. Where the treasure was concerned he had always been the most reliable of my champions. But we had never become close, and we had no mutual friends who could help me find him. I telephoned him constantly, with no result. No one knew of his whereabouts; his offices were occupied by new tenants; and I began to suspect the worst. I have never heard of him to this day. He loathed publicity, and his one dream was to retire to that farm in South Australia with his horse for a companion. I hope he may have achieved it.

In my uncertainty and disappointment I began to lurch from bar to bar on a drinking spree, and this was to lead to my next adventure. In a Singapore yacht club I was to meet my next backer, Barry Whelan, also an Australian. But before we came to an agreement I made another acquaintance who was to prove of considerable interest to me in the future. He was an American called Bill Mathers, and he had a yacht of his own in the basin. For a few days he seemed interested in the possibility of providing the new backing I needed.

Cut to July 1984. A month before I was released from prison in Ho Chi Minh City, Bill Mathers and his yacht *Soo Fong* were apprehended off the south coast of Vietnam. Bill was arrested along with a motley crew which consisted of an Australian, a Frenchman, two women and a child. They were detained and interrogated and imprisoned, exactly the same fate as had happened to me, and they were still in prison after my release. The two women and the child were released in early 1985 and the rest of the crew a little later. All had to pay the same 10,000 dollar fine. Bill Mathers was released in mid-1985, when I caught up with him by chance in Singapore again. The story he told me on this occasion was that he was rounding the tip of South Vietnam in the *Soo Fong* on the way to Hong Kong when he was arrested by a patrol boat off some islands east of Ca Mau Peninsula, thirty miles off the Vietnam coast. He said he spent the first few weeks in a military compound and was then permitted to live on his yacht under guard at Can Toi. In the last few weeks of detention he lived in a small hotel in Can Toi.

Mathers had several business interests in Singapore and told me that while he was under arrest he was pressured by the Vietnamese to become an economic spy for them. They wanted him to sign documents to that effect and tempted him by offering to return his very expensive yacht and by waiving the fine. In the end he was forced to leave *Soo Fong* and all the sophisticated equipment on board in Vietnam.

Naturally enough I double-checked Mathers' story in Singapore, while he went back to America saying he was leaving the Far East permanently. Other sources told me that before he sailed in 1984 he had been looking around for crew, including professional divers, and taking on board some very expensive and advanced equipment. Putting two and two together, I assumed he was also after Kidd's treasure, though I had been careful not to tell him that I had already found some on our original meeting.

The man I eventually took as my backer, Barry Whelan, did not have a boat of his own. Barry was a big, open, fresh-faced blond Aussie, much more immediately to my liking than Duncan had been. I took to him at once, and at first sight I thought him more trustworthy even than Duncan. He was an altogether different character. Barry was a gregarious fellow. He bought his own drinks and he had his own buddies. Some of them were quite peculiar. There was one in particular, a huge ex-US Marine who had served in Vietnam. He had sparkling eyes and a gungho manner, and his enthusiasms could be quite dangerous. After a few drinks he loved to impress people by producing his gun and sticking it between your eyes and saying he knew how to use it. He used to wear big high-heeled fancy boots, which fascinated me until I knew the reason why he wore them. One day, after several rounds of drinks, I turned round in a bar and there he was with a knife at my throat. He kept it down his boots.

There are a lot of madcap ex-servicemen in that part of the world just waiting to have another go, but Barry was a much quieter type. He was married to a Singapore girl and lived in a respectable bungalow in the suburbs. When I told him I had Kidd's maps and I believed I could find the treasure, he took an intelligent interest. Of course I didn't tell him that I had found some already, only that I was sure I knew where to look. The first cache was still for me and Duncan when he turned up. At that point I still held out hope that his disappearance was only temporary. I had made up my mind to go back for the second cache.

There was only one trouble. Barry was not rich. In fact he was employed by a Singapore company, and his typical thrifty Chinese Singapore wife probably had many better plans for his salary than giving it to me. Barry asked me how much it would cost. From my experience mounting the first expedition I could say straight off 6,000 dollars and 1,000 for any emergency. Barry brought the money to me in cash, 14,000 Singapore dollars. It was a good omen. Added to that, I already had a crew. Jean-Pierre Maumont was a young Frenchman who had put a notice on the board at the Changi Sailing Club asking for adventurous seasonal employment. We met, and I liked him. We decided that he should go straight to Songkla in Thailand to look for a suitable boat and I would head for Bangkok on the same mission.

It was obvious to me that I was not going to go back to Trengannu. The local Malays would have been far too intrigued to see me turn up again hell-bent on one of my bizarre adventures. The story I had told them worked a treat the first time and had met with success against all the odds; all the same, these were poor people whose boats were their only means of livelihood, and to them my adventures were of paramount interest. I decided I needed someone else to go with me this time, someone who was more used to the idea that boats sailed as far as Vietnamese waters. I knew exactly who this was because I had met them while I was there – the Thai fishermen.

The obvious place to look for a boat in Bangkok was the dock area, about thirty miles from the main town and pretty seamy even as such places go. I found it fascinating, but there was no doubt it could also be dangerous. You could get your throat cut as a foreigner in these parts, and no one would ever be any the wiser. I decided to take a taxi, keep it waiting and stroll round the quays just to see what sort of craft were berthed there. Around on one of the back quays I found just the sort of Thai boat which had inter-cepted me on the high seas, with a captain who looked rather more friendly than most, considering he can't have been used to seeing tourists. He smiled at me and I got round to asking him where he was going. He said nowhere for the next few days. We had established that he spoke English. Soon he was joined on deck by the crew, and they in turn came down on to the quay to speak with me. I suggested a drink, they eagerly took up my offer, and we all went off to a café. We ordered beer for me and Thai whisky for them, a heady brew which is cheap and which they much prefer. In the café I asked the captain how near he went to the Vietnam coast and he said twenty to thirty miles. I asked him whether he would consider taking along some passengers. He indicated that he might well.

We had established a principle, but I didn't feel like getting down to the finer points with the language barrier. We arranged to meet again and I went back to Bangkok, where I had a brainwave. I rang up one of the many escort agencies in the town. The place is famous for them. I asked them if they had a girl. They had nothing but – in all shapes and sizes – but I wanted something special, a girl who spoke impeccable English.

Lek and I met in the lobby of the Hotel Nana. I wasn't staying there, but it was a good meeting place. I didn't want her to come to my hotel because I wanted to keep my movements as secret as possible. Lek was not a beautiful girl but she did indeed speak good English. She seemed to have had quite a good education. I realized that she might find my proposition difficult. The dock area was no place for a girl in her profession, who would immediately be taken for granted. I said I would pay her twice her usual fee. The fee set by the escort agencies is about 1,000 *baht* for an evening – about 50 dollars – that is quite apart from any extras which might take place behind closed doors. I said I would give her 2,000 and a big tip. I said I had some business with a Thai sea captain called Ciao King. We would take a taxi to the docks and keep it waiting.

My cautious approach to the evening turned out to be quite justified. As the driver took us through a hangar in the dock area we were surrounded by about six scoundrels who were clearly about to drag Lek from the car and force her on to their boat. I said we were looking for Ciao King. It was a potentially dangerous situation in which I, her escort, spoke not one word of their language and they spoke none of mine. The eight Thais, including Lek and the taxi driver, hammered out their argument while I urged the driver to carry on. Fortunately we were rescued in the nick of time by the sudden arrival on the scene of Ciao King. It was quite a relief, and the three of us, Ciao King, Lek and I went to the café for a drink and light meal.

The proposition I was going to make to him was that I wanted to photograph Vietnamese boat people leaving

168

their country. I said I wanted to bring a friend along and a dinghy so that we could penetrate Vietnamese territorial waters relatively discreetly and asked him if he would drop us off the Vietnamese coast and come back for us two or three days later. He agreed to all this and even proposed that we should clinch the deal in his own home on a future occasion. Ciao King was a likable man and at this point I decided it was more interesting to both of us if he knew a little of my real intentions. I told him I knew of an island where treasure might be buried and that there would be a cut of it for him in return for the safe passage there and back of myself and a friend. I spread out my navigation chart and showed him where I wanted to go.

Taking him into my confidence was not as foolhardy as it might seem. I had already established in the nicest possible way that I had influential friends in Thailand who were monitoring my voyage and suggested that he would be answerable to them ultimately. But it was his invitation to visit his family which really loosened my tongue. I have always found it a pleasure, anywhere, in any country in the world, to visit the homes of local people, no matter how poor, and I had learned one thing in doing it. The poorer they are, the prouder they are. To receive you behind closed doors involves a certain mutual loyalty and trust. Ciao King was no different in this from anyone else. He lived in a ramshackle one-storey hut with his wife and six children, and though the family were poorly dressed and we all sat round on the floor, they still possessed a stereo, a television and fridge. Thai whisky was served and beer especially for me, which was a great honour because it is quite expensive. Ciao's wife served fried fish on a platter to go with it.

We were not quite at the point of home visits that evening in the café, but our relationship was already progressing well. We were all in a good mood from the whisky, and Lek, my escort, was confident of her tip and perhaps even a little extra business before she went home. But just at that point a most beautiful Thai girl entered the little place on her own, looked around and sat by herself at a far table. She was exquisite. I couldn't take my eyes off her and I couldn't imagine what she might be doing alone in a rough place like this. In the end I had to ask her. 'What do you do for a living?' I said. Her reply in perfect English left no room for doubt. 'I sell my body,' she said. I was fascinated with her and rather rudely, under the influence of drink, spent half an hour talking and flirting with her at another table. I promised to phone her. My official escort was pretty irate when I returned to her table. 'But you are with me,' she said. Perhaps if I had had less to drink I would have remembered my manners, but as it was I was obsessed with the beautiful girl. She plied her trade in the simplest of back-street rooms with just a bed, a dressing table and a mirror.

Ciao King was scheduled to depart almost immediately. I asked him if he could give me four days to arrange my side of the trip. He was his own master and moreover was holding a deposit from me by this time. Jean-Pierre came down from Songkla, where he had no luck finding a boat and joined me in Bangkok, where I was able to tell him my good news. But before we could depart there was still the problem of the dinghy. The obvious place to buy one was in one of two big marine suppliers, opposite the main post office. From there I was referred to another boating supply shop and was in the process of fixing up a second-hand dinghy which was more within the means of Barry Whelan when I returned to see Ciao King at the docks forty-eight hours later. He, his boat and my deposit were gone.

Almost immediately I found another fisherman with a boat. I negotiated without the aid of the escort agency this time, and this time I did not make the mistake of parting with my *baht*. We went through the same routine, the drinks in the café, the visit to his wife and family, we pored over the navigation chart together and I promised him 10 per cent of the treasure for himself and 20 per cent to divide amongst his crew.

The Bangkok fishermen's methods of doing business were reminiscent of Awi's in Malaysia. Everything took twice as long as it should. 'No problem, no problem,' was always on their tongues, but in the end one always seemed to crop up. I was getting used to this by now, and I knew that the excuses these people made when things did not work out were never the real ones but were about face-saving. I think this man said his wife was going to have a baby. Jean-Pierre and I drowned our sorrows on Soi Cowboy, the street of American-style saloon bars. It was becoming clear that Bangkok had nothing else to offer us, so we went south to Pattaya beach, where I had a contact number from one of the marine shops where I had looked for a dinghy. In this way I met Mr Muk.

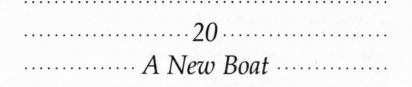

20
A New Boat

It was by now May 1983, the spring weather was delightful, and anyone in Pattaya with nothing else on their mind was certain to have a good holiday. It is a typical Far Eastern resort with sandy beach shaded by palm trees, a gentle ocean offering water sports, and plenty of bars offering beautiful girls. Jean-Pierre and I checked into the Sun and Sand, a small hotel a little back from the beach. We went out with the girls, swam a little and lazed around, but we also took buses and taxis up and down the stretch of coast trying to find the elusive boat we needed.

Muk was the Mr Fixit of the area just as Awi had been in Trengannu. He was a dependable man, married with a host of kids, and he lived with his family in a nearby fishing village in a little house right on the water's edge, its living room standing in the sea on stilts. I told him I wanted to have a boat at my disposal for a couple of weeks, and he immediately produced a tiny ramshackle tub with motor and cabin but barely thirty feet long. We tried it out up and down the coast. It was perfect for puttering but far too unstable for what we wanted and it definitely lacked the aura of dependability. This disappointment was finally too much for Jean-Pierre, who announced his intention of going back to Bangkok. I was sorry to see him go, but I did not try to dissuade him. It had been a pleasant interlude for him – a fully paid month's holiday at Barry Whelan's expense.

Muk continued to look for dependable craft with more space in them while I decided to devote my time to finding a dinghy. For all the water sports in Pattaya, there was none. You could have scooters or surf boards or pedaloes, but no dinghies which measured anything like the twelve feet I needed. Fifteen miles to the north of Pattaya, how-

172

ever, there was a much less Europeanized resort which seemed to have the very thing. Whole extended Thai families came here and crowded into a boat for the afternoon. I located a perfect twelve-foot fibreglass craft and kept my eye on it for the time being.

Meanwhile I came across Mr Song. He was a Thai layabout who cottoned on to the western tourists and took pride in coming up with what they wanted. I didn't trust him as much as Mr Muk, but he had the great advantage of speaking good English. I told him I wanted some crew. Together we toured the little port areas and interviewed fishermen. As usual there were days of delay while the deals were discussed, but finally Song picked on two fishermen whose names sounded very much like Mr Tea and Mr Beer. Song, Tea, Beer and I used to meet in the garden of the Meridian Hotel overlooking the sandy beach to plan the second expedition to Hon Tre Lon. They knew exactly what they were getting into. I laid out the navigation charts and Song was offered 5 per cent for his part in interpreting the whole venture. The two Thais were on 10 per cent each.

I was not keen about taking the two Thais into Vietnamese waters, where they would be in unnecessary danger, so I envisaged a plan whereby they would stay in the gulf and we would communicate with walkie-talkies that I had brought with me from Singapore. They had a range of about twenty miles, which meant that Tea and Beer could ride safely at anchor until I needed them to rendezvous with me and, hopefully, the second cache, which I had already located, and perhaps further deposits of Kidd's treasure. There was one snag. Neither spoke a word of English and they did not seem inclined to learn. I was making very little progress with my Thai. Song came up with the answer. He wrote down a sheet of signals which we all had to learn by heart – though the sheet was also to be pinned up in the cabin, to be on the safe side. I learned the numbers one to six in Thai, and each number had an equivalent message. No. 1 was: Okay, we have the treasure and we are on our way back. No. 2 was: We don't have the treasure but we are coming back anyway. No. 3 was: We have been delayed, please wait. And so on.

We still had no boat, but things were working out to my advantage. It was getting to be the quiet season on Pattaya beach and it was a buyer's market. I re-approached Muk, who proved able to find a better fishing vessel than the first in return for 15 per cent of the treasure and 1,000 US dollars boat hire. He was very businesslike about this and insisted that a proper contract be drawn up with his solicitor. The boat was made ready and Tea and Beer were put in charge of loading it with provisions – all the heavy work I had had to do on my own back in Trengannu. It was left to me to find an extra crew member – and a dinghy. I had had so many disappointments with young guys who seemed to be game but then dropped out when the going got a bit tough that I decided I needed someone with a bit of a track record.

There was one name I knew which seemed to fit the bill: John Everingham. Everingham was a bit of a legend in these parts. He owned a café in Bangkok. He was an Australian married to a beautiful Laotian girl whom he had rescued from the war-zone by swimming across the Mekong River to get her. I had read about his exploits in *Reader's Digest*, and it seemed that he might be game for another adventure. I got his telephone number from the news agency Reuters, and rang him out of the blue. He agreed to meet me and discuss the venture, but his heart was not in it. His current life-style suited him perfectly. It was he who first mentioned to me Fred Graham, the young American who finally came with me. He was up country at the moment trying to find stories to start a career as a photo-journalist. Everingham did not know how to contact him but promised he would let him know my whereabouts if he turned up in Bangkok.

Just two days before I was planning to leave Pattaya there was a knock on my bedroom door in the Sun and Sand. Fred Graham was indeed young, just eighteen and a half at the time. He was very tall, about six foot one, with mousy fair hair and carrying a lot of puppyfat. I liked him immediately but I don't suppose I would have told him all about the trip so quickly if I had not had the boat and the rest of the crew ready and waiting and wanted to leave as soon as

possible. I showed Fred my maps and charts and asked
him if he was interested in coming along. Fred, who was
committed to his career in journalism, was primarily interested in getting a good story. He was never entirely sure
whether that meant he had to come all the way to the island
with me and actually disembark and try to dig up the treasure with all the dangers that that entailed. I offered him
10–15 per cent of the treasure if he went right through with
the trip. He hesitated. I asked him what he wanted and he
said all the newspaper and press rights.

I smiled half-heartedly. I had spent four months preparing for this trip and his demand was plainly impossible.
He suggested a sixty-forty split in my favour. My mind was
too occupied thinking over the final details to argue, but I
told him on no account would I part with any book or film
rights. He agreed and went placidly off to Bangkok to get
his cameras and films, saying he would join me at the hotel
the next morning. His youth was an advantage when it
came down to it, and for the time being I was pleased to
have a western companion. As with Barry Whelan, I did
not tell Fred or the two Thais that I had already recovered
treasure from the island which was our goal. I didn't know
Fred, and I feared he might easily have been persuaded
by the two Thais, who were carrying weapons, to force me
at gun-point once at sea and make me take them down the
gulf and reveal the location of the first cache.

Now everything was ready but for the dinghy. I went to
see my friend on Pattaya beach, paid him a deposit and
signed for the boat, saying I was going to hire it for a week.
Naturally I didn't want him to know that I would be sailing
300 miles to Vietnam with his dinghy during that week.
For the time being he took me out in the boat and showed
me how the 35-horsepower motor worked. It had a five-
gallon tank and I asked him how many miles it did to the
gallon. He said about four or five. I casually looked in the
tank and saw that it was about three-quarters full and calculated that we had been out for half an hour. After we had
tried the dinghy out I told him I would return that afternoon with an American tourist friend and we might take a

couple of girls out with us. That was an acceptable way of relaxing in Pattaya.

Fred rolled up at the hotel at lunchtime. The two Thais had taken a taxi to Bang Sari, where they would do a few last jobs on their boat, and it was left to me to find the girls. During the preceding few weeks I had been frequenting a bar-restaurant which had girls just up the road. It was owned by a Thai with a Californian wife. At lunchtime I went to see her and explained that a friend and I would be taking a dinghy out for an hour later that afternoon and that we would like to take a couple of girls with us. She said she could supply two and I agreed to give them 200 *baht* each.

At five o'clock Fred and I turned up at the bar, picked up the girls and got down to the beach. The fellow had the dinghy ready, complete with a full tank. Fred was rather reserved, and I urged him to play the part by putting his arm round one of the girls and giving her a kiss or two.

We headed out beyond the bay about a mile with them and gradually moved around the headland to the south. I was afraid the owner could still see us if he was looking. Once out of sight we pulled in at a hotel beach about a quarter of a mile along the coast. We took the girls for a drink, and then we told them the sea was obviously getting too rough for them to return to Pattaya beach with us in the boat.

Several months later, at one of my 'interviews' with the Vietnamese security officials, I learned that the Thai government was particularly concerned about these two girls. They were not known personally to the dinghy owner, and when the news of our disappearance came out, it was assumed that the girls had come on the trip with us. Not at all. I paid them and gave them their taxi fare back to Pattaya, and when they had gone, Fred and I took the dinghy way down the coast the eighteen miles to Muk's house with its protruding jetty at Bang Sari. We just made it with the contents of the five-gallon tank. It was an uncomfortable ride pitching and banging in the dark, in a pretty rough sea, and at first we couldn't find Muk. Then we checked into the only hotel in the place and went out with Muk for a drink before turning in quite early at ten p.m. The next day we would be off.

There was still a bit to do before we were on our way. Muk had had the contract prepared by his solicitor and we stepped over to his office first thing and signed it. Then we went to the local petrol station and picked up enough petrol for the trip and took it to the boat.

It was a bigger boat than on my first trip with a similar superstructure and another number rather than a name. The dinghy had a name. It was called *Boy*. It was written in big white letters on a yellow background. It was much heavier and larger than the first dinghy and impossible for one man to haul on board by himself. In the end we decided to tow it from behind. Tea and Beer had taken my shopping list and filled the holds with enough cans and fruit juice for Fred and myself and sacks of rice for them. I noticed that they had also stocked up on Thai whisky for themselves. I provided the equipment for digging and reconnoitring and one other thing – a home-made Vietnamese flag. Painstakingly Fred had sewed a yellow star on to red material. As a matter of fact I had made one myself for the first trip but I never had occasion to use it.

If Muk was being careful and far-sighted, so was I. In exchange for my signature on his legal contract I handed him a letter for Barry Whelan with instructions to post it to Singapore. To Barry I said that if he didn't hear from me in eighteen days he was to contact the British Embassy, all the coastguards in the area, but first of all Mr Muk. My previous trip had made me cautious and I knew some of the hazards that could befall me.

I didn't suspect that the very first hazard would be the Thai whisky. By the time we had rounded the point of Sattahip, Tea and Beer were well into their first bottle. There was no problem so far. We steamed at about eight knots due east for some four hours when suddenly a heavy sea started running from the south towards Rayong. Equally suddenly I learned that Tea and Beer were in no condition to steer. The first I realized about the drinking was when the boat nearly capsized as they turned it sideways into the trough of the wave.

I had never been out with Tea and Beer myself before, but I had been told by Muk, who had shown them the ropes off his bay, that they were experienced sailors. I had only been out once with Muk when he showed me the boat, but I knew what to do. I wrenched the wheel from the Thai sailors and steered the boat into the wind and the waves.

I was very clear-headed and excited to be on my way. Fred was not quite so sure. He had doubts about how far he would accompany me. The Thais appeared to have sobered up with the shock and I let them steer again, but the same thing happened just a little while later.

At about ten p.m. it became too rough to carry on and I decided to put out the anchor about twenty miles off Rayong. There was no point in pushing on in this condition. The Thais slept well and woke feeling apparently fit, but the sea was still rough. Considering the weather I decided not to chance it any further out, and we crept along the coast for about fifteen miles towards the island of Ko Samit, where I knew there would be some shelter. There was clearly work to be done before we embarked on the serious stuff. Fred had to make up his mind whether he was coming along, and the Thais had to adopt a sense of discipline. Apart from their drinking habits, I realized they had cheated me over the provisions and, more importantly, over the fuel we had on board. If we hit a lot of rough weather or had to go out of our way I was doubtful if we would have enough. Ko Samit is a little tourist island where I figured we might take more on board and put a few other things right. For one thing, it had rained during the night and the roof was leaking over the cabin and dripping into the sleeping area. That would have to be fixed with the plastic sheets I had had the foresight to provide.

We pulled up in a sheltered area about 100 yards out into a bay fringed with little chalet dwellings, and after resting, eating and sorting a few things out, Beer, Fred and I untied the dinghy and rowed in to the shore. We pulled it up on the beach and went for a walk to investigate the facilities. We were told there was no fuel in this particular area and were redirected elsewhere. We had a coke in a little café before starting back to the mother boat just as dusk was falling. On this expedition, like the last, I had decided not to use lights. Though there were hazards involved, on the whole it was better because no questions need be asked. This evening I was to discover the hard way about one of the hazards. We couldn't find Tea and the boat.

We left the beach in the dinghy and headed into the pitch-black night in the direction of our fishing boat, but there was a strong current running, and without realizing it we must have moved quite a distance beyond it. We turned back again and missed it again. We must have motored round and round in circles for about half an hour, encountering strong tide and current, looking for the dark shape which would mean the boat. It was no good. I decided we would have to wait until daybreak. Finally we headed further along to some lights on shore where there were some small holiday chalets and took one of the chalets to sleep in at a cost of one dollar a night each. The backpackers in this part of the world love little paradise islands like this where the accommodation is so cheap they can linger in an open-ended idyll. Another time I might have joined them, but as it was I was irritated by this introduction, keen to get everything ship-shape and press on with my adventure.

I woke at daybreak, roused the others, and we all breakfasted briefly on bread and coffee. The mother ship was nowhere to be seen and the dinghy appeared to be lying much higher up the beach than the night before. When I looked out at the bay my heart turned over. Everywhere black jagged rocks were thrusting out of the blue water. The landscape had changed beyond recognition since the previous evening. The tide had gone right out. We launched the dinghy and soon found the boat about 300 yards away in a cove which was not visible from the chalets. As we teetered towards it I realized we had had a very narrow escape the previous night. Our outboard must have only just cleared the vicious rocks which the tide had uncovered. It was a miracle that we had not ripped the bottom of the boat or smashed the propeller and been carried out to sea by the current. I took it as a good omen, but I am not sure that I should have done.

We spent the early morning putting the plastic sheeting on the roof and hammering it down. The incident the night before had done nothing for Fred's mood, and I asked him to make a positive decision whether or not he wanted to come along, otherwise I would put him ashore and he could wait for passage back to Bangkok. He decided to come along. The sea was calm and I decided not to stay around to look for fuel. I didn't want another incident with the rocks; time was pressing and I estimated we had just about enough fuel. Besides, with Tea and Beer aboard there was another way of refuelling – from any one of the fishing boats we were bound to meet in the gulf. We weighed anchor at ten a.m. and carried on more or less on the same easterly course ten miles off the coast till that evening we were twenty miles from the Cambodian border. The die was cast. Of course it was necessary to keep well away from the war area. We would turn south into the open sea.

We steamed on into the night for a couple of hours before we saw the red lights following us. From its speed and manoeuvrability and the dogged way in which it pursued us I concluded it was a patrol boat. It was a testing situation, for I had no idea which nationality it was, though I figured it was almost certainly Thai. The only sensible course was for us to carry on and hope that she would get bored. She was a tenacious thing and it was four hours before she slipped off into the night and we could be reasonably sure we had thrown her off. Here again it was good to have the Thais on board. After the first euphoria of putting out to sea they seemed to have abandoned their drinking habits and were quietly taking it in turns to steer the boat and to keep house on the aft deck. There they would make a little fire and boil pans of rice at every meal. With four of us we could take turns at the helm, taking watch and turning in. There was no need to anchor to sleep, which was just as well, for we were right out in the gulf in deep water. By the time morning came we were sixty miles from land and we curved round due east, heading for Vietnam.

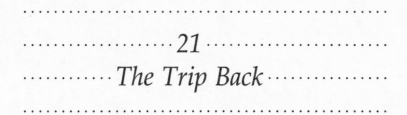

From the outset the trip back was by no means plain sailing. The first thing that happened was a little skirmish with a Thai fishing vessel which kept cutting across our bows, having a good look at us, steaming off in the direction of home, and then curling around to come back as if it had forgotten something. Again I was aware of the advantage of having Thais on board. If the boat had stopped us, the chances were that Tea and Beer's natural wit with their fellow Thais would steer us away from any confrontation. I was feeling much more confident than at the same point on the first trip and was beginning to look forward to getting back to my island.

But the dangers were not over yet. Again that night, sixty miles out of Cambodian waters, we were followed by a patrol boat. This time it was a modern one with bright flashing lights. The boat zig-zagged in pursuit of us for nearly two hours and I had plenty of time to wonder what would happen if it caught us and if, as I feared, it was Cambodian. I was familiar with the war zone from my first trip to Thailand when I was looking for a boat along that coast, and I did not want to get any closer to it than that first experience. All the atrocious images which filled the newspapers during the Cambodian Pol Pot era come to mind.

From the point of view of shipping this second trip was proving much more eventful than my solo voyage had been. We were on the principal Bangkok–China, Hong Kong–Philippines sailing lines, and we were navigating only with a small five-dollar compass. On my first trip the boat had a big built-in compass, though I took a spare one along. On the third day, as we turned towards Vietnam, another fishing boat appeared to the north, this time either

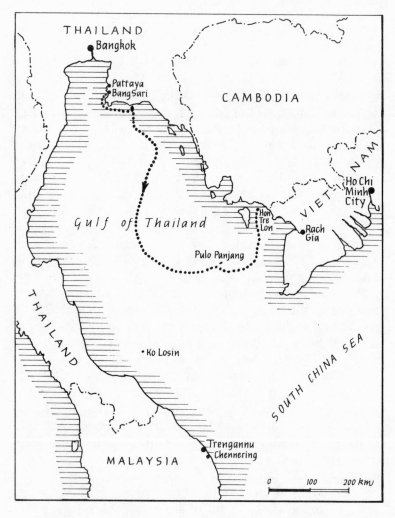

Richard Knight's second trip to Hon Tre Lon

Thai or Cambodian, and again very interested in our activities. We skirted round it, we changed direction; but it turned and followed us for at least an hour. I was growing distinctly uncomfortable, but Tea and Beer seemed to be taking it all in their stride; after all we had nothing to hide, yet. Fred, always a phlegmatic soul, was at the wheel and quite calm. I had to prod him to keep up the speed so we could outrun our pursuers. I was nervous because I remembered what had happened when I was on my own. I didn't want to lose the cameras this time, Fred's professional Canon and my rather simpler model and the Instamatic. I didn't want to lose the equipment, which they might well find if they got curious and realized we had no nets on board.

The weather at least was in our favour. The sea was calm, there was a light warm breeze, and giving the little boat all she had we were able to outrun the fishing vessel by about five o'clock at night. It was just two hours later and starting to get dark when we saw Pulo Panjang, the island with the radar station on its peak, lying dead ahead. I knew where I was. It was a good feeling. We had been right out in the gulf, without islands or landsights, and I knew we were bearing down on it at an angle sixty degrees different from the first time. There was no mistaking that high tip in these parts. I took a circular route to the south-east, knowing we would soon be safe in the darkness. At that point we were joined by a school of dolphins playing round the boat, and Fred said it was a good omen. We immediately turned due east, and by early morning we could turn north towards Pulo Dama. That night we cruised very slowly to conserve fuel. It was dead calm.

We came across only one fishing boat all the next day. We had used more fuel than I bargained for steering a devious course this way and that down the gulf to avoid the previous ones. I was seriously worried about the amount of diesel fuel left for the mother ship, though we had enough petrol for the dinghy to get to Hon Tre Lon. As long as Tea and Beer were going to be left on their own, we ought to do it soon, when they could cut back into open waters and stop one of their own countrymen and take some more fuel on board. Still things were going smoothly with no patrol boats and fishing vessels in sight. At dawn we turned in a north-easterly direction. The peak of Pulo Dama came up around three p.m.

At five p.m. we were twenty miles south of Pulo Dama, and we started to put everything on board the dinghy which we had towed all the way from Bang Sari. At this point, as we were loading the dinghy, I asked Fred if he wanted to join me – or remain on the mother ship. It took about five minutes before he decided to come. Now we unhitched it and set out into calm seas with 120 litres of petrol to make the sixty-mile dash for Hon Tre Lon. We arranged to meet the Thais in seventy-two hours, and we each took a walkie-talkie with us. They set off into inter-national waters, hopefully to find the fuel they needed.

Our first fright was the sight of a huge Vietnamese boat coming straight over the horizon to the east. I was scanning the horizon through binoculars, and there was no mistak-ing its country of origin. On either side of the prow it sported the black and white eye on a red background. Within a very short time it became clear that neither of us wanted to gain ground on the other. We were watching each other like two frightened animals. In the event the Vietnamese boat made the first move. Despite its huge bulk it turned back on itself and disappeared over the horizon. I realized the captain had concluded we were a pirate vessel and was even more afraid than we were. It was unquestion-ably a refugee boat.

There was worse ahead. No sooner had we lost the boat than our outboard motor broke down, although we had tested it before cutting loose. Our own mother ship was nowhere to be seen. We figured it was useless calling it at this juncture. We tried everything we knew to get this motor started, and luckily Fred knew more than I did. It was no good. It refused to budge. After an hour we were very discouraged. It was eight o'clock and there was nothing to do but resign ourselves to a night drifting and bobbing around on the open sea. We decided to make it as pleasant as possible in the circumstances and set to unpack-ing some of the food we had with us. Then we dossed down on the seats at the bottom of the boat fighting for space with the provisions and the fuel.

It was a very uncomfortable night and I was glad to see the light, even though we were now vulnerable again from alien shipping. Fred immediately started tinkering with the motor, but the damn thing still refused to respond. I could still see the tip of Pulo Dama, but it was obvious we had drifted away from our course in the night. We had to find our bearings and get moving in the right direction. There was only one thing for it. We would have to row the twenty-odd miles to Pulo Dama. It would be a terrible challenge, and we would be the easy prey of any boat which cared to stop us. There was simply nothing else we could do. For the time being there was no one in view, and I resolved to get moving while this was still the case. I drew comfort from the fact that during the last trip I had made a dash back with the treasure in full daylight passing through exactly this same area and seen no one. That time, of course, I had a motor. It was then that I realized we didn't even have a complete set of oars. We had lost one of them somewhere between Thailand and Vietnam, probably in the heavy seas we had had at the beginning of the trip. The voyage was beginning to look ill-starred, but I was not ready to give up. We slipped the remaining oar in the row-lock and took the spade which was destined to uncover the treasure and slipped it in the other. Fred rowed with the spade and I used the oar. The system was not perfect and we spent a bit of time flailing around trying to get the two in synch. Finally we had some sort of stroke going but it was useless against the tide, which was bringing us further and further south. Fred went back to the engine. It still wouldn't budge. I was beginning to resign myself to drifting aimlessly for a couple of days until the mother ship was somewhere near and hoping we would be able to contact it with our walkie-talkies. Then suddenly I heard the put-put of the outboard. Fred had fixed it. We were getting on very well at this point, and this stroke of success put me in a good mood, as did the inventiveness which led him to tie a piece of string on to the speed governor and hold it all the way through the journey. We still had the question

185

whether we should go forwards to the island, backwards towards the rendezvous point, or stay more or less put, seeking out some shelter until dark. We had lost eighteen hours at this stage so I thought there was nothing for it but to take the chance and to push on in case we were sighted and picked up by a patrol boat. I reasoned we might just as well pursue our objective, because we were vulnerable either way.

Fred had a fast lick out of the motor now, and we set out to round Pulo Dama to the left when we saw a fishing boat on the horizon. We veered east immediately, dipping out of its sight, and carried on for about eight miles till we saw another vessel. This time I feared it would be a patrol boat. Back we went to the left. It was frustrating but at fifteen knots our light craft was capable of outrunning any fishing boat, which would be capable of only half that.

We were still forty miles from Hon Tre Lon. Five miles further on behind Pulo Dama there was another fishing boat. This time the best way of escaping detection was to plough straight on through the Pulo Dama islands group. It didn't follow us; indeed after about half an hour it was lost to sight; all the same I was sure it had seen us, and I wondered about the consequences.

By now we were about one and a half hours away from the island. We could go straight in to Hon Tre Lon, or we could make for Pulo Ceci again and shelter there. I considered that for a bit, but there was also a fishing boat some distance to the west and we would have to pass well within its sight to do that. We were getting very short of time and we would have lost another six to eight hours waiting at Pulo Ceci till after dark. There was also possibly not enough fuel, allowing for our return trip out. I chose the straight run, and there were no further interruptions. I was very excited. Then we saw them, the Pirate Island group, and there in the background Grand Pirate Island, as Hon Tre Lon is called on the French charts. It was two o'clock in the afternoon, and its wooded eastern tip loomed out of the water to the north offering shade and sanctuary from the fierce sun. As we neared the island we passed a couple of tiny local fishing boats carrying one or two islanders and nets. There was no hiding from them and nothing for it but to try and allay their curiosity. I waved to indicate we were on a friendly mission. We had towels over our heads and kept low. The dinghy must have looked unusual to them, but they might have taken us for a Vietnamese patrol boat.

We arrived at three p.m. on the north-west tip of the island, a place I had never seen in daylight but was fairly confident was uninhabited. There was a beautiful beach in the shelter of a tiny island joined to the mainland by a sandy isthmus. Its causeway was about ten yards wide and covered with coconut palms and low-lying shrubs. It seemed like paradise after all we had been through. Just as I had done the first time, we dragged the boat out of the water and hid it under some of the bushes. Although it was made of fibreglass it was too heavy to drag very far. Its yellow hull blended in with the sand, but we took the precaution of covering it up with green plastic sheets which served as a sort of camouflage in the jungly surroundings. We were very tired but determined to get on our way and started unloading the equipment and provisions and making a base camp about thirty yards on to the island. Only when we had done that did we rest and have a bite to eat in the shade. We were both very elated, but our high spirits were a little dampened by the knowledge that we had been seen by the locals. Would they mount a search party, and if so when? I kept turning these things over in my mind, hoping that perhaps we had been too far away and looked too weatherbeaten for our obviously European features to be in focus.

Fred had the nonchalance of youth. He started taking photographs of everything in sight and encouraging me to press on to find the treasure area while it was still light. We walked over towards the northern ridge through thick vegetation to see how far we were from the valley, but the terrain was difficult and I knew we would not be able to make it before nightfall, which was due in an hour and a half. It took me some time to persuade him of the wisdom of waiting till the next day. In the circumstances it was too dangerous to spend the night exposed in the open valley.

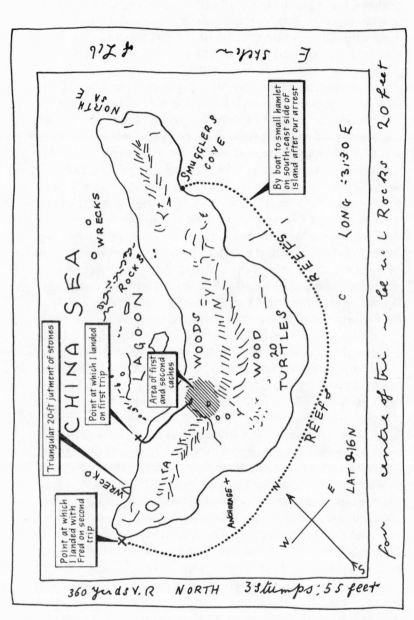

Kidd's map of his island, with notes added by Richard Knight

Fred was restless. Treasure island was too much of a temptation to him in all sorts of ways. Suddenly he turned his
attention to the coconut palms which were laden with fruit
above our heads. He set out to climb one of them. As he
did so I turned and looked across the isthmus to another
little island we had passed about four hundred yards away.
There were two little boats riding at anchor to the leeward,
and if they were looking that way their occupants could
not fail to see Fred silhouetted up the tree in the light of
the dying sun. I told him to get down. If they spotted him
they would know he was a westerner in his Californian
shorts. I was very glad when it got dark. It was a relief
when Fred resigned himself to the idea that he must wait
till tomorrow to see the treasure and lay down under the
bushes on the isthmus on the groundsheets and sacks we
had brought from the boat. I sat and watched the dying
sun go down till there was just a thin strip of light on the
horizon.

It was a beautiful night but hot, and I decided to go for
a swim before turning in. I splashed in the shallow water
for just over five minutes, dried myself and lay down close
to Fred. I started to drift off into sleep, and then a sudden
feeling made me sit bolt upright. I listened and stood up.
There was nothing, and yet . . . I decided I must be imagin-
ing things. There were the outlines of the twelve coconut
palms, and there amongst them two new silhouettes,
black, man-size stumps. One quivered slightly. They were
men. But who were they? Villagers or guards? Instinctively
I raised my hands above my head just in case . . .

At that moment a torch was flashed on me from behind
a tree ten yards to my right. Immediately several rounds
of rifle fire were loosed on us. About eight or ten young
Vietnamese guards shouting a babble of commands
advanced rapidly towards us. Within seconds they were
tying our hands behind our backs, using our own pink-
coloured straw string. Even in the heat of the moment I
remember thinking that looked rather comic sprouting out
of Fred's back. For twenty minutes we stood there while
they hunted around for other possible intruders, loosing
off gunfire as they did so and finding in the process most
of our equipment.

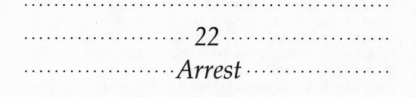
I stood face to face with Vietnamese security officials. 'You are under arrest. What are you doing on this island?' 'I am looking for buried treasure.' It was an incredible story; no wonder they refused to believe me and marched me off to jail. You know the rest and how I paid for my return to the island with fourteen months' imprisonment, not to mention the months I spent in Saigon quite alone knowing that Fred Graham was already back home in California. I began to feel like Papillon, a desperate prisoner in an alien land, and dream up impossible ways of escape when even death sometimes seemed preferable to another night behind bars. I was counting the days if not the hours, wondering whether I would ever be released. The American hostages were in Teheran for 444 days. I began to think I would break that record.

In the end it was 432. That was the point at which a British-born taxi-driver, Kenneth Crutchlow, who had emigrated to California, came up with the rest of my release fund. It was a truly altruistic gesture and to this day I do not know quite why he should have made it. On my release he even made the trip to Paris to meet with me when I finally landed in the west. I had left Vietnam for England forty-eight hours before, taking the long route, just as I usually seem to do, this time via Hanoi, Bombay, Moscow and Paris. It was the cheapest passage I could get and cost £415, which was paid for by the Foreign Office and reimbursed from the fund. It also avoided Bangkok. The British Embassy did not want me to land there, as they knew I faced possible arrest. They were still looking for *Boy*, the dinghy.

Kenneth Crutchlow never argued terms before he put down the £6,000 which brought Buster Gray's fund up to the 10,000 dollars stipulated by the Vietnamese government. I regretted not being able to tell him the truth of finding a cache on my first trip. He was very publicity-prone, and the two Thais were still in Vietnam. I promised him I would tell all at a later date.

That is almost the end of the story – but not quite. When I go back this time there will be no mystery about the whereabouts of the treasure at all. The first cache is in a hiding-place known only to me on the coast of the Gulf of Thailand. The second is marked by an auger hole on Hon Tre Lon itself. And the third and fourth caches – at least I know where *not* to look.

Both times I had been on the island under my own auspices it had been a brief visit, with barely time to look around, but after about a month in jail the Vietnamese authorities invited me to show them where the treasure was. Instead of asking me to write down my life story at the interviews and confess that I was a spy, they started producing the navigation charts and the Kidd charts they had confiscated from me when they first arrested me. No pirate stories seemed to have filtered down through their own national history, and they knew nothing of Captain Kidd.

First they asked me all about him and where I had found the maps. I told them the whole story about that. Then they asked me where the treasure was. Here I had to be careful. It is what I had guessed might happen, and I was prepared for it. I resolved then I would take them more or less to the right area, which was obvious anyhow, but at all costs avoid the right spots. It was eighteen months since I had filled in the hole after finding the first cache, and in all probability it would be overgrown and not noticeable.

The second cache might still have evidence of the auger hole which I had drilled. If they noticed it and put two and two together I would have some explaining to do. It could have been fatal. They had also said I would shortly be released, and this is what I desperately wanted. I didn't want to be too specific, but I also knew I could not throw them off the scent by being uncooperative without getting myself in worse trouble. I told them the vague area in which

I said I believed the treasure could be found, indicating the western part of the island. They were anxious for much more detail and wanted to know why I had come to this conclusion, so I translated the legend around the map. Then they asked me whether I had ever been on the island before they caught me. I said no. They asked me if I would like to go to the east of the island and again I said no, though I did not understand the significance of the question at the time.

Three days later my interviewer brought to our meeting my metal detector. The authorities had obviously examined it and were unsure of how it worked. He did not seem to have any understanding what it was and thought it was some sort of spy device. He wanted to know exactly how it worked and why, and whether it had any other function. Then about a week after that I heard the guards clanking up the prison staircase to my room before daylight. It must have been about four o'clock in the morning. It was the first time this had happened and it scared the living daylights out of me. That night I hadn't slept well and I had already been up and taken a dip in the blocked footbath and allowed myself to dry off in the general stuffiness of the cell.

Suddenly the door opened. It was my interpreter. 'Put your clothes on,' he ordered. Then he offered me a cigarette to put me at my ease. He came back twenty minutes later and ushered me downstairs to a car which was waiting in the courtyard with two guards in it already. We joined them and the car drove into the centre of Saigon through the Chinese area, which I could just make out, and then to the other side of the city and out into the open countryside. It was getting light, and it was obvious that we were going south – back to Rach Gia, where we arrived about six hours later. There I was put in the same prison cell which had been mine when we were first arrested. The interpreter visited me briefly and said we would leave first thing next morning. All through the day I had not dared ask him where we were going to, but now I felt I had the answer. We were going back to the island.

The next morning we made an even earlier start. The car

192

arrived at 3.30 and with it six guards. We were all driven
to the quay, where there was plenty of military activity,
and I was left alone in the car while they attended to some
last-minute details. There in the water about forty yards
away I could just make out the dark outline of a naval boat.
It looked like a gunboat from the shape I could see at the
front. Half an hour later I was on it. I was led down to a
cabin towards the rear of the ship with four sleeping berths
and several portholes, and I was locked in. At about five
in the morning we left, and we were at sea for most of
the day. I was beginning to enjoy this temporary taste of
freedom now it was obvious where I was being taken. I
could leave my cabin escorted to go to the head, which
measured about one yard square and was located right at
the front of the ship. There were six chickens in it.

The boat was an old American gunboat, about seventy
feet, which had seen better days. I had a chance to get a
good look at it when I was brought up on deck after we put
down anchor. We were about 200 yards off Grand Pirate
Island. I recognized the place: we were in Smugglers' Cove.
I tried to let my eyes play over it without any sign of recognition, because my interpreter immediately took up position beside me and asked me if that was the island I had
described. 'I suppose so,' I answered carefully. For the
unforeseeable future we would live on the boat while by
day we would search the island for Captain Kidd's treasure. The small wooden boats were already rowing out from
the village to welcome us and take us ashore.

That first day we landed halfway through the afternoon
and I was taken straight back to the guardhouse which had
been my first stop the night we were arrested. There I was
presented to a three-star Viet Cong colonel, an obvious war
veteran since he was about forty-five years old. He was
sitting at a table in the guardhouse and in his way was
perfectly pleasant, though he shared those hard North
Vietnamese features which seemed to be common to all the
officials in the country. Tea in a pot was brought and cups
and we were subjected to a photo session which all the
villagers watched with great interest. First Mr Lee, the
interpreter, photographed us, and then I was photo-

graphed with Lee. A top-grade intelligence officer was also present.

Then we set out on a tour of the island, heading first towards the north. I relaxed at this point, because I could genuinely say even under duress that I had never been in these parts before. A little path had been trodden through the undergrowth surrounded by banana trees. Two soldiers with rifles at the ready and hand grenades in their belts went ahead; I followed on with the interpreter, while the rear was brought up by two more soldiers, the colonel, the intelligence officer and the photographer, who told me later that though he was only thirty he had been in the army for eighteen years. We walked down on to the sandy beach, where we broke open some coconuts and sat down to drink their milk. 'Now you take us where you want,' they said. 'Tomorrow we will give you back your camera and you may photograph whatever you like.' While I was sitting I was aware they were watching my every movement, looking to see where I turned my head and where my gaze came to rest. My eyes wandered along the road leading up from the jetty and up the contours of the eastern hill, and I could sense their tension as they did so. There right on the top was a tiny military installation. It was only a little brick look-out, about four yards square, but it obviously had some significance to them. That is why they had asked me whether I was interested in the east of the island. I turned my gaze away quickly. To think I had carried out both my expeditions under the eyes of the Communist guard permanently installed on one of the highest points of the island!

I got up and started to walk along the beach in the other direction – towards the treasure area. Now I was really feeling guilty, for I was in an area I knew well, but I was stumbling around pretending this was all brand-new to me. But strangely enough the guards seemed to tire of the activity before I did. After an hour they announced we would go back to the ship and rest. After the rest we weighed anchor and made a tour of the island, which allowed me to see exactly the lie of the land as Kidd had drawn it.

Once aboard a friendly routine was established. I ate by myself at the back of the boat, and I discovered the chickens were for me. There was one less every day I went to the head. I had a staple diet of chicken and chicken soup padded out with potatoes. Meanwhile a bodyguard sat in front of me and watched me eat. Even if I wasn't hungry he would pressure me to finish it off. I was allowed to swim off the side of the boat – they even handed me my swimming trunks, which they had confiscated that first night – but if I swam my bodyguard swam too. I thought briefly of escape, but it seemed to be out of the question under these circumstances. There was one plan which seemed to have more mileage than the rest. If I went up to the head at the front of the boat after dark I could easily slip quietly overboard. It meant a drop of about five feet from the deck level. I would swim underwater for about fifteen yards and away into the blackness. I reckoned my absence would only be noticed after about five or seven minutes, which would give me time to get about 200 yards from the ship in any direction. They would be at a disadvantage because they simply wouldn't know, and although they had torches they had no spotlight. Even if they started the engine and pulled up the anchor, the best they could do would be wander round in circles looking for me.

What would I be doing? I would either swim to the island itself, about 200 yards away, or across to one of the others in the group, which would not be more than half a mile. Each was about half a mile long, with a couple of native dwellings on each and lots of places to hide. I could have stolen one of the inhabitants' small fishing boats and paddled away. This was where my plans hit trouble. The distance to international waters was at least fifty miles, and I would never have made it by daybreak. I might have reached the Pulo Dama islands, but they would certainly send out a boat for me, or several, from the small naval base at the south end of Phu Quoc. There was another problem too. In such an unstable ten- or twelve-foot boat I would never stand much chance in the open sea unless the weather were calmer than the proverbial millpond.

Reluctantly I decided once more that I had to wait out my sentence.

The evenings meanwhile were quite pleasant. After our meal we would sit on the front gunwale in the darkness, and Mr Lee would join us and the six soldiers and the Viet Cong colonel. The only person who was conspicuously absent was the intelligence officer, who used to go ashore by night and chat up the women. The rest of us sat in a circle as if we were at a party, and we would talk about our two countries. 'Tell me about England,' the colonel would start. 'Which part are you from?' The questions had a political bias and I was sure they still thought I was American. 'We threw out the Americans,' he would say. 'And the French and the Japanese. We are independent.' But they also had a personal flavour. 'Do you like alcohol?' the colonel asked, apologizing for the fact that there was no beer. He gave me a cigarette instead, and told me he had never been married.

In the morning I got up to a bowl of chicken soup and was taken back to the guardhouse on shore. There they handed me Fred's camera. It was a sophisticated 2,000-dollar thing and I had no idea how to use it, so they simply took it away again. Then they asked me where I wanted to go. Once more the soldiers with guns and hand grenades at the ready led the curious procession, this time along the south beach where, on Kidd's map, turtles played. The interpreter was carrying the copy of *The Money Pit Mystery* which I had with me at the time I was arrested. Lee asked me what a turtle was and I explained, and the next thing I knew the intelligence chief and two soldiers peeled off from the main party and came back with a two-foot animal which had been caught the other day. They bought it from a villager. Everyone was then photographed holding it.

We walked along to the point on Kidd's map marked 'anchorage', and this became our base for the next three lunchtimes. It was surrounded by poor shacks which sheltered the Vietnamese families which lived on the island. One was occupied by a pretty Vietnamese woman with a small child who prepared lunch for our party. After lunch we lay down and rested on a wooden bed in the shade of the huts. Our timetable was quite leisurely. I was always allowed to swim. But sooner or later I was called to duty. Where did we go from here, they wanted to know.

I took the party up from the anchorage into the valley where I knew the second cache was, and about two thirds of the way up I got out the metal detector. This piece of equipment was to entertain them for hours. They thought it was very sophisticated and they were very careful about assembling it and cosseting it. I walked around with it occasionally getting a slight reading but showing no great enthusiasm. Then after about half an hour I figured they were looking for some progress. 'Let's try digging here,' I said. At this point four Viet Cong soldiers stripped to the waist. They took the best part of an hour to make a hole four feet deep with the interpreter and the intelligence officer hovering around saying: 'Are you sure this is the right spot?' When we had reached two feet we broke for lunch. 'It would be much deeper than this,' I said. I helped them dig from time to time, but I was not expected to do the heavy work. Before lunch I was allowed to rest in the shade of the woman's hut. I think they left me there on purpose to see whether I really could communicate after all in Vietnamese. I was careful not to even try, though I would have liked to chat the girl up. When I looked round I saw one of the soldiers resting with his hand on his pistol. It was a warning not to behave rashly in any way.

Anyway I had quite enough on my mind deciding just how far I could string the Viet Cong along. I wanted them to abandon hope of finding the three caches I was certain were buried still and write me off as a crank. I did not want them to conclude I was a spy, which would have been wrong, or wilfully obstructive, which would have been right. In the afternoon I decided to display signs of growing frustration and abandon the first hole. We started on another, but by four o'clock they were quite ready to pack up and start the hour-long walk back to the village. By five they wanted me back on the boat so I could not escape under cover of darkness. They never seemed dismayed by not finding anything, much less than I was by the idea of us stumbling on the third and fourth caches. I was terrified too that someone might spot the auger hole I had made in the second. I had no idea how long this was all going to go on, the poring over the aerial photographs they had taken from the mother ship, the inspection of the ground for clues, the surveying, the digging, the friendly eleven a.m. break for the first coconut. How long could their humour last?

It went on for four days. On the fourth we pulled up the anchor at midday and went away, hooting the villagers with the ship's siren as we left. I stood on deck and bade farewell to my island – but perhaps not for ever. When I was not identifying with the American hostages and Papillon in jail I imagined myself as the Count of Monte Cristo who had a treasure waiting for him when he got out. That was the thought that kept me going.

Much as I bitterly regretted returning to the island during my long period in the Vietnamese prison, I knew I had one sure chunk of Kidd's treasure to look forward to when I got out. That was the first cache which I had recovered and buried on the Gulf of Thailand. Around the time Fred Graham was released I was so desperate to get out myself and so depressed by prison life that I wrote a letter to the Vietnamese authorities asking to be taken back to the island again. My plan was to allow them to stumble on the second cache this time, accidentally on purpose. I was sure they would release me then, but in the event they did not take up the offer.

That means the bulk of the treasure is still there, and thanks to the Vietnamese themselves I now know Hon Tre Lon blindfold. I haven't altogether given up the idea of returning for the second, third and fourth caches. As for the first, my plans are already well advanced for its recovery in Thailand.